INSIGHT FOR LIVING

——— Broadcast Schedule ———

Shedding Light on Our Dark Side

May 22–July 2, 2001

Tuesday	**May 22**	**Shedding Light on Our Dark Side** *Selected Scriptures*
Wednesday	**May 23**	**Shedding Light on Our Dark Side**
Thursday	**May 24**	**Shedding Light on Our Dark Side**
Friday	**May 25**	**Pride: The Absence of Humility** *Selected Scriptures*
Monday	**May 28**	**Pride: The Absence of Humility**
Tuesday	**May 29**	**Pride: The Absence of Humility**
Wednesday	**May 30**	**Lust: Sex Out of Control** *Selected Scriptures*
Thursday	**May 31**	**Lust: Sex Out of Control**
Friday	**June 1**	**Lust: Sex Out of Control**
Monday	**June 4**	**In Defense of the Helpless** *Selected Scriptures*
Tuesday	**June 5**	**In Defense of the Helpless**
Wednesday	**June 6**	**In Defense of the Helpless**
Thursday	**June 7**	**Special Interview with Dave Carder**
Friday	**June 8**	**Special Interview with Dave Carder**
Monday	**June 11**	**A Careful Analysis of the Unborn** *Psalm 139:13–18*
Tuesday	**June 12**	**A Careful Analysis of the Unborn**
Wednesday	**June 13**	**Celebrate the Feast!** *1 Corinthians 5:6–8*
Thursday	**June 14**	**Celebrate the Feast!**

Friday	**June 15**	**Curing the Plague of Death** *Ecclesiastes 3; Romans 5*
Monday	**June 18**	**Curing the Plague of Death**
Tuesday	**June 19**	**Claiming the Promise of Life** *Acts 2:22–38*
Wednesday	**June 20**	**Claiming the Promise of Life**
Thursday	**June 21**	**Life's Turning Points** *Acts 9:1–22*
Friday	**June 22**	**Life's Turning Points**
Monday	**June 25**	**The Turning Point of God's Sovereignty** *Daniel 4; Romans 11:33–36*
Tuesday	**June 26**	**The Turning Point of God's Sovereignty**
Wednesday	**June 27**	**Deliverance from Despair** *Selected Scriptures*
Thursday	**June 28**	**Deliverance from Despair**
Friday	**June 29**	**God's Amazing Grace** *Selected Scriptures*
Monday	**July 2**	**God's Amazing Grace**

Broadcast schedule is subject to change without notice.

Insight for Living • Post Office Box 69000, Anaheim, CA 92817-0900
Insight for Living Ministries • Post Office Box 2510, Vancouver, BC, Canada V6B 3W7
Insight for Living, Inc. • 20 Albert Street, Blackburn, VIC 3130, Australia
Printed in the United States of America

Shedding Light on Our Dark Side

From the Bible-Teaching Ministry of
Charles R. Swindoll

INSIGHT FOR LIVING

Charles R. Swindoll graduated in 1963 from Dallas Theological Seminary, where he now serves as the school's fourth president, helping to prepare a new generation of men and women for the ministry. Chuck has served in pastorates in three states: Massachusetts, Texas, and California, including almost twenty-three years at the First Evangelical Free Church in Fullerton, California. He is currently senior pastor of Stonebriar Community Church in Frisco, Texas, north of Dallas. His sermon messages have been aired over radio since 1979 as the *Insight for Living* broadcast. A best-selling author, he has written numerous books and booklets on many subjects.

Based on the outlines and transcripts of Chuck's sermons, the study guide text is written by Lee Hough, a graduate of the University of Texas at Arlington and Dallas Theological Seminary. He also wrote the Living Insights sections.

Editor in Chief:
Cynthia Swindoll

Study Guide Writer:
Lee Hough

Assistant Editor:
Wendy Peterson

Copy Editors:
Deborah Gibbs
Cheryl Gilmore
Glenda Schlahta

Designer:
Gary Lett

Publishing System Specialist:
Bob Haskins

Director, Communications Division:
Deedee Snyder

Manager, Creative Services:
Alene Cooper

Project Supervisor:
Susan Nelson

Print Production Manager:
John Norton

Unless otherwise identified, all Scripture references are from the New American Standard Bible, © The Lockman Foundation 1960, 1962, 1963, 1968, 1971, 1972, 1973, 1975, 1977. Used by permission.

Scripture taken from the Holy Bible, New International Version, Copyright © 1973, 1978, 1984 International Bible Society, used by permission of Zondervan Bible Publishers [NIV]. The other translation cited is J. B. Phillips: The New Testament in Modern English [PHILLIPS].

An effort has been made to locate sources and obtain permission where necessary for the quotations used in this book. In the event of any unintentional omission, a modification will gladly be incorporated in future printings.

ISBN 1-57972-200-8
Cover Design: Michael Standlee Design
Cover Photograph: © Steve Greenberg/Index Stock Imagery, 2001
Printed in the United States of America

CONTENTS

INTRODUCTION

Have you ever had the glorious feeling of being so close, so in love with the Lord that Peter's bold words became your own? "Even though all may fall away, yet I will not." We've all experienced emotions and thoughts like that and they're wonderful. The Apostle is not the only one whose passionate faith—"I'm ready to go both to prison and death for you"—bordered on the braggadocio. I've been there; I know the invincibility he felt. Perhaps you're feeling that way now.

But then there's the dark side of Peter's denial. Not long after he had declared his loyalty-to-the-end speech, calamity struck and fissures of doubt suddenly penetrated the impregnable. "I'll never fall away" quickly crumbled into "I never knew the man." The man's impressive-sounding, rock-like faith was shattered by shameful denial.

I hope you never know that experience. But if you don't, you will be the exception rather than the rule. Virtually every Christian I've known can remember a time in his or her spiritual pilgrimage when a falling-away has occurred. How can that be? you may wonder. How could a Christian, who is saved from sin, turn around and serve sin?

All too easy, I'm afraid. You see, we all share the same dark side as Peter. It's called a sin nature, that natural tendency within even the holiest of saints to rebel against God. Follow me as I explore the back alleys of our dark side with the lamp of God's Word. Together let's confront the painful reality of our own sinfulness with the reassuring light of Christ's forgiveness and power to overcome whatever we may find. Light, remember, has one primary purpose: to dispel darkness.

Chuck Swindoll

Charles R. Swindoll

PUTTING TRUTH INTO ACTION

K nowledge apart from application falls short of God's desire for His children. He wants us to apply what we learn so that we will change and grow. This Bible study guide was prepared with these goals in mind. As you go through the following pages, we hope your desire to discover biblical truth will grow as your understanding of God's Word increases, and that you will be encouraged to apply what you've learned.

To assist you in your study, we've included a section called Living Insights at the end of each lesson. These exercises will challenge you to study further and to think of specific ways to put your discoveries into action.

There are many ways to use this guide—in personal devotions, group studies, discussions with friends and family, and Sunday school classes. And, of course, it's an ideal study aid when you're listening to its corresponding *Insight for Living* radio series.

To benefit most from this Bible study guide, we would encourage you to consider it a spiritual journal. That's why we've included space in the Living Insights for recording your thoughts and discoveries. We hope you'll return to those sections often for review and encouragement as you continue to grow in your walk with Christ.

Insight for Living

Shedding Light on Our Dark Side

Chapter 1

SHEDDING LIGHT ON OUR DARK SIDE

Selected Scriptures

> Prone to wander, Lord, I feel it,
> Prone to leave the God I love;
> Here's my heart, O take and seal it;
> Seal it for Thy courts above.[1]

C enturies have passed since Robert Robinson wrote those lyrics, and yet they still have a relevant ring about them today. For each time we lift up those words in worship, we proclaim an important truth that sheds light on our dark side; namely, that all of us are prone to wander into that wilderness called sin . . . yes, even those who follow God fervently.

Now some of you may be wondering, How can we be prone to wander and be committed followers at the same time? Doesn't God somehow protect His children from the encroachment of sin? Many seem to think so, including the unsaved who read about a believer's fall and sometimes sneer, "And I thought he or she claimed to be a Christian!" What they're implying, of course, is that if this person were a true Christian, he or she would never sin.

Never sin? Is that what it takes to be a Christian—perfection? Surely not, or none of us would qualify. Are we saying, then, that it's OK to sin, that it's inevitable and we should just accept it? No, not that either. Then what?

As you can see and have probably encountered, confusion clouds many people's minds concerning the Christian's relationship

---

1. Robert Robinson, "Come Thou Fount of Every Blessing," in *The Hymnal for Worship and Celebration* (Waco, Tex.: Word Music, 1986), no. 2.

to sin. And to be honest, it can be downright bewildering, especially in light of such paradoxical lyrics as "Prone to leave the God I love."

To dispel some of that confusion and shed a little light on our dark side, let's turn our attention to three clarifying comments.

Some Clarifying Remarks about the Christian and Sin

First, *becoming a Christian is not synonymous with becoming a model of perfection.* You've probably seen the bumper sticker that says: Christians Aren't Perfect, Just Forgiven. Believe it or not, that's pretty good theology. You see, when we trusted Christ for salvation, our identity was changed, but not our sin nature. We were once citizens of darkness under Satan's dominion; now we belong to Christ and are citizens of heaven (compare Eph. 2:1–3 with Phil. 3:20). As citizens, we are declared righteous on the basis of our faith in Christ, but that doesn't mean we have reached perfection.[2] So our citizenship may have changed, but that tendency inside each of us to behave as if we were still subject to the prince of darkness has not.

Our destiny has also changed, but again, this has not affected our natural propensity to sin. At the moment of conversion, God irrevocably sealed us to Himself for eternity with His Spirit (Eph. 1:13–14). He is our passport from hell to heaven. Yet even though our destiny is secure, that in no way qualifies us to pose for a portrait of the perfect person. Though ultimately defeated, the flesh—our sin nature—continually fights to keep us under its influence rather than the Spirit's. The apostle Paul reminds us of this conflict in Galatians 5.

> The flesh sets its desire against the Spirit, and the
> Spirit against the flesh; for these are in opposition
> to one another, so that you may not do the things
> that you please. (v. 17)

God has taken care of the vertical changes concerning our identity and destiny, but it is still our responsibility and choice to obey Him in the horizontal sphere of daily living.

Second, *remaining sinners by nature means we can become sinners in practice.* It stands to reason that if it's in our nature to wander, then wandering will certainly be in our actions too. The deep-seated desire to sin that's inside each of us is impossible to hide. We may

---

2. See Romans 4:1–5; 10:10; 2 Corinthians 5:21; and Philippians 3:8–9.

2

not admit it; we may call it by other names; we may even delude ourselves into thinking it doesn't exist—but it's always there, always revealing itself through immorality, conceit, greed, sensuality, strife, jealousy, outbursts of anger, arrogance, envying, drunkenness, and much more (see Gal. 5:19–21; 2 Tim. 3:1–5).

If this weren't enough to convince some, the blunt words of the apostle John leave no doubt.

> If we say that we have no sin, we are deceiving ourselves, and the truth is not in us. (1 John 1:8)

Third, *living above the practice of sin is not automatic.* In Romans, Paul makes it clear that Christians can overcome sin to walk in fellowship with God—but it doesn't just happen. Note the specific instructions he gives on how to be "dead to sin, but alive to God."

> If we have become united with [Christ] in the likeness of His death, certainly we shall be also in the likeness of His resurrection, *knowing* this, that our old self was crucified with Him, that our body of sin might be done away with, that we should no longer be slaves to sin; for he who has died is freed from sin. Now if we have died with Christ, we believe that we shall also live with Him, knowing that Christ, having been raised from the dead, is never to die again; death no longer is master over Him. For the death that He died, He died to sin, once for all; but the life that He lives, He lives to God. Even so *consider* yourselves to be dead to sin, but alive to God in Christ Jesus.
>
> Therefore do not let sin reign in your mortal body that you should obey its lust, and do not go on presenting the members of your body to sin as instruments of unrighteousness; but *present* yourselves to God as those alive from the dead, and your members as instruments of righteousness to God. (6:5–13, emphasis added)

Distilled into one paragraph, the three essential steps Paul encourages might read something like this: Operating on the basis of what the Scriptures say (knowing the truth), plus realizing that we are free from sin's grip (considering it a reality), we are able to live in the realm of victory (presenting ourselves to God) on a daily basis.

Key Questions That Deserve an Answer

As clarifying as these first three comments may be, they've probably raised some questions in your mind whose answers aren't very clear. So let's continue shedding light on our dark side by answering five illuminating questions.

1. What Happens When Christians Sin?

In Ephesians 5:15, Paul exhorts, "Be careful how you walk, not as unwise men, but as wise" (see also Col. 2:6). He then goes on to describe what it means to walk wisely:

- understanding the will of God (Eph. 5:17)

- not getting drunk (v. 18a)

- being filled with the Spirit (v. 18b)

- making melody in our hearts to the Lord (v. 19)

- giving thanks to the Father out of a grateful heart (v. 20)

- having a humble, teachable spirit (v. 21)

When we stumble and fall because of sin, however, that fellowship we've enjoyed while walking in obedience to Him is broken. Sin grieves the Spirit of God and quenches the manifestation of His power in us (see Eph. 4:30; 1 Thess. 5:19). Our spiritual vitality wanes and our bodies suffer the consequences, just as David once lamented:

> When I kept silent about my sin, my body wasted
> away
> Through my groaning all day long.
> For day and night Thy hand was heavy upon me;
> My vitality was drained away as with the fever
> heat of summer. (Ps. 32:3–4)

This can happen when you or I sin. But be careful not to confuse loss of fellowship with loss of salvation. Nowhere do the Scriptures teach that Christians can lose the precious gift of their identity and destiny in Christ because of sin. David demonstrated this when he sought to mend his broken fellowship through confession rather than praying to be saved a second time (v. 5). He was eager to walk with God again, to experience the joy and intimacy that came from following in his Father's footsteps. So he wrote,

> Restore to me the joy of Thy salvation,
> And sustain me with a willing spirit. (Ps. 51:12)

2. Is It Possible for Christians to Be Enslaved to Sin?

Paul tells us in Ephesians 2:1–2 that before becoming Christians, each of us walked "according to the course of this world, according to the prince of the power of the air." We were Satan's subjects, sons and daughters of disobedience. Through faith in Christ, however, we became children of God, set free from our bitter bondage to sin. That's wonderful news, of course, but we must still face one sobering question: Even though we have been freed from sin's domination, can we allow ourselves to become enslaved by it once again? The implied answer in Romans 6:12 is clearly yes.

> Do not let sin reign in your mortal body that you
> should obey its lusts.

A little further in this chapter, the Apostle reinforces this same idea:

> You *belong* to the power which you choose to obey,
> whether you choose sin, whose reward is death, or
> God, obedience to whom means the reward of
> righteousness. (v. 16b PHILLIPS)

Slavery to sin results in a deathlike existence; one that could possibly even lead to addictions and risks that result in physical death. "Sinful habits are hard to break," writes Jay Adams in his book *Competent to Counsel,*

> but if they are not broken they will bind the client
> ever more tightly. He is held fast by these ropes of
> his own sin. He finds that sin spirals in a downward
> cycle, pulling him along. He is captured and tied up
> by sin's ever-tightening cords.[3]

Interestingly, Paul refers to this kind of carnal condition as "walking like mere men" (1 Cor. 3:3). The Spirit can empower the believer to obey God and walk in newness of life, but He will not force that on us. Which path we will walk is a choice we must make each day.

---

3. Jay E. Adams, *Competent to Counsel* (Phillipsburg, N.J.: Presbyterian and Reformed Publishing Co., 1970), p. 145.

3. Does Sin Have Power over Christians?

This next question closely parallels the previous one. The subtle difference has to do with the issue of power. As Christians, we know that we can become enslaved to sin if we obey its lusts instead of obeying God. When this happens, does that give sin power to control us? Again, if you read Romans 6:16–18, the answer is clearly yes. But mark this well—the power sin wields is limited. It doesn't have the power to change our position in Christ, our eternal destiny, or identity; it can only influence our temporal condition, how we live today.

That sin can impact us, powerfully so, is evidenced in Paul's anguished cry. "For the good that I wish, I do not do; but I practice the very evil that I do not wish. . . . Wretched man that I am! Who will set me free from the body of this death?" (Rom. 7:19, 24). And his answer? "Thanks be to God through Jesus Christ our Lord!" (v. 25a). Through Christ's death and resurrection, we have not only been set free from eternal death—separation from God—but also from sin's power to control our daily lives. The same Spirit who raised Jesus from the dead now lives in us to make our spirits alive (see 8:1–17). We've been given a heavenly power; but, as with enslavement, it is still a matter of choice, our choice, as to whose power we will obey.

4. How Can Christians Recover and Walk in Victory?

It wouldn't be all that helpful to examine the Christian and sin without touching on this last question. All of us have experienced defeat when it comes to sin. Perhaps even now one or two besetting vices have gained a powerful foothold in your life. Is it possible to recover and redirect your steps to follow God in these areas? . . . yes, YES, YES!

Regardless of how far you've strayed, how deep the pit you've fallen into, or how powerful sin's pull may feel, there is hope. The One who utterly destroyed sin's grip to give you eternal life can also empower you to live the abundant life that blossoms under His guidance. Changing sinful patterns of thinking and living may take time, but Jesus is on your side, and He is willing to help, just as Paul once wrote:

> If God is for us, who is against us? He who did not spare His own Son, but delivered Him up for us all, how will He not also with Him freely give us all things? (Rom. 8:31b–32; see also 1 John 4:4)

Though every situation has its unique set of problems and circumstances, if we're to restore our fellowship with the Lord, these biblical steps are essential. The first principle is found in Proverbs 28.

> He who conceals his transgressions will not prosper,
> But he who confesses and forsakes them will find
>   compassion. (v. 13)

When we've sinned, our natural reaction is to hide our mistake, just as Adam and Eve tried to do by cowering behind some trees. Rather than conceal our mistakes with excuses or blame, however, we're to openly admit them (see Ps. 32:5).

This may not be easy—the consequences of our sin can be terribly hard to endure. Confession is not a cure-all. The wounds sin inflicts can go deep in ourselves and others and often require time to fully heal. But confession is always followed by God's instant and complete forgiveness, and our second step toward restoration is to accept the clean slate He hands us.

> If we confess our sins, He is faithful and righteous
> to forgive us our sins and to cleanse us from all
> unrighteousness. (1 John 1:9)

Last, we need to walk again in the light as God Himself is in the light. For if we do, "we have fellowship with one another, and the blood of Jesus His Son cleanses us from all sin" (v. 7).

5. Are There Some Techniques That Will Help?

Expanding a little further on what we've just said, here are four practical insights for maintaining your walk with Christ.

First, *keep short accounts with God.* As soon as you realize you are getting off course, confess it and reset your compass to follow Him. Time is no friend when you're going the wrong way.

Second, *stay in close touch with God's people.* When sin burrows into our lifestyle, we typically back off from our Christian friends and anything that reminds us of our sinfulness. If you find yourself pulling away, take a close look at what's pulling and in what direction!

Third, *refuse to rationalize wrong.* When you do something wrong, confess it—don't cover it up. And if it injures others, ask for their forgiveness and take responsibility for the consequences you have caused.

Fourth, *learn to say no by practicing the word every day.* Sin is stealthy—and relentless. Learning to tell it no will break its power before it breaks you.

"Prone to wander, Lord, I feel it, / Prone to leave the God I love." That's our dark side. Hopefully, we've shed enough light to not only give you a better look at it, but also to help you know and love the Light of the World more deeply. If that's true for you, then commit yourself to Him with the last two lines from Robinson's lyrical prayer:

> Here's my heart, O take and seal it;
> Seal it for Thy courts above.

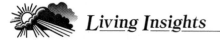 **Living Insights**

Discussing the painful reality of the Christian and sin is not easy. Many believers treat the subject as some sort of dark family secret, something taboo that good Christians don't talk about. Why? Because we'd like to think that no Christian would ever molest a child; we'd like to believe that all pastors are pure and never commit adultery; we wish that no born-again believer would abuse a spouse or buy pornography or embezzle money. But in the real world, many have done these things and are doing them right now—and that frightens us, confuses us, makes us angry and unsure.

What do we do? For those who can't handle the mess of Christians committing such sins, the solution to the problem seems simple: just deny that these people were ever saved to begin with. Cast them out of the fold as black sheep who don't belong. Make them scapegoats who must bear the wrath for everyone's closeted sins. Now's the chance to do a little spring-cleaning and restore a nice, neat Christian world where no one ever dirties himself or herself with anything more than a few white lies.

Oh, if only life were that simple, that clear-cut and clean. But the truth is, sin muddies us all, Christian and non-Christian alike. It doesn't make distinctions; it doesn't play favorites, reserving its worst for the lost. It comes after everybody to darken all that it can.

Take a moment to closely examine how sin infiltrated the lives of several prominent people in the Scriptures—two of whom are mentioned in the hall of faith in Hebrews 11. Read the passages listed, then note under the appropriate headings from our lesson in what way each person specifically opened the door to sin by violating the safeguards we've been learning.

8

Samson (Judges 13–16)
Eli (1 Samuel 2:12–3:14)
Saul (1 Samuel 15)
David (2 Samuel 11:1–12:14)
Ananias and Sapphira (Acts 4:32–5:10)

Keep Short Accounts with God

_____   _____

_____   _____

Stay in Close Touch with God's People

_____   _____

_____   _____

Refuse to Rationalize Wrong

_____   _____

_____   _____

Learn to Say No by Practicing Every Day

_____   _____

_____   _____

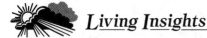 *Living Insights* _____ STUDY TWO

"Nathan then said to David, 'You are the man!'" (2 Sam. 12:7a).

Who can forget the prophet's sobering words that brought David's sin with Bathsheba into the open where it could no longer be denied. What's even more sobering is that God could probably stand a Nathan before many of us as well. For we are cut from the same bolt of sinful humanity as David. Did he love God? Yes, passionately. And yet he also committed adultery and murder. It happened, and something similar could just as easily happen to either you or me.

Has sin gained a foothold in any area of your life? Has some doubtful practice taken control? Take a moment to examine your own life as you did the lives of David, Samson, and the others in the first Living Insight. See where you may be failing, consider which of the four biblical principles listed need to be strengthened, and then probe for some practical solutions using the following space to write out your thoughts.

Keep Short Accounts with God

_____

_____

_____

_____

Stay in Close Touch with God's People

_____

_____

_____

_____

Refuse to Rationalize Wrong

_____

_____

_____

_____

Learn to Say No by Practicing Every Day

_____

_____

_____

_____

Chapter 2

PRIDE:
THE ABSENCE OF HUMILITY
Selected Scriptures

Throughout Church history, only seven sins have earned the right to be called deadly: pride, greed, lust, envy, gluttony, anger, and sloth. Each is extremely dangerous, not only because of the destruction it wreaks but because of its insidious ability to deceive. Perhaps, though, none is more treacherous than pride. It's the leader of the pack, you might say, the proud parent of gluttony, greed, and the other unholy offspring who were raised on its milk of selfishness.

But they are not her only children. We, too, bear her resemblance. We, too, were suckled on selfishness. We've grown up with envy and lust; they're family. Pride encourages that kind of a close-knit bond. Even after we break all family ties with this deadly sin through faith in Christ, pride continually beckons us to come back into the fold and embrace it once again. And the sad fact is, many of us do every day.

It would probably strengthen our resolve to resist pride if we could see it for the evil that it really is. To do that, let's begin by examining a few characteristics common to all seven cardinal sins.

Initial Remarks about "the Seven Deadly Sins"

The term *sin* in its original and most basic biblical definition means "to miss the mark." That mark is righteousness based on God's holy character. So when we sin, in any capacity, we fail to hit His mark. In that sense, all sins are equally wrong. However, this does not mean that all sins are equal. Let's explore why.

First, *all sins are wrong . . . but some are more damaging than others.* Consider the sin of worry, for example. If not taken to an extreme, it hurts no one except the worrier and can be tolerated much more easily than, say, the sins of greed or lust. By comparison, those two felonies make worry seem like a misdemeanor.

Second, *all sins are wrong . . . but a few are absolutely deadly.* The lethal wrongs we commit not only devastate our reputation and relationships, they also sell us out to enslavement and a life of bondage. But that's not all. Deadly sins initiate other sins as well. Greed, for example, is a capital sin because it can motivate us to steal, lie, or oppress others to satisfy its demands. Envy is a capital sin because it can breed suspicion and violence to get what it wants. Lust ranks among the worst because it dehumanizes and puts self-satisfaction above all else.

If not stopped, each of these cold-blooded killers will set in motion disastrous consequences. As Solomon Schimmel writes in his book *The Seven Deadly Sins:*

> Every deadly sin fuels harmful social phenomena: lust—pornography; gluttony—substance abuse; envy —terrorism; anger—violence; sloth—indifference to the pain and suffering of others; greed—abuse of public trust; and pride—discrimination.[1]

Third, *all sins are wrong . . . but the deadly sins can make others as miserable as they make us.* The effects of some acts of disobedience can be contained within the narrow perimeter of our own private worlds. The wrecking-ball presence of these deadly sins, however, bashes beyond our boundaries into the lives of others. Schimmel adds:

> All of us are engaged to one degree or another in a personal, ongoing battle with sin and vice. . . . Although our anger doesn't make most of us murderers, our lust doesn't make most of us rapists, and our greed and envy don't make most of us outright criminals, they, together with gluttony, arrogance, and sloth, often make us and those who have to live with us miserable.[2]

Biblical Analysis and Evaluation of Pride

Now let's single out pride from the others for a more in-depth study.

What Is It and Where Did It Start?

In answer to the first half of the question, pride is conceit,

---

1. Solomon Schimmel, *The Seven Deadly Sins: Jewish, Christian, and Classical Reflections on Human Nature* (New York, N.Y.: Macmillan, The Free Press, 1992), p. 4.

2. Schimmel, *Seven Deadly Sins*, pp. 3–4.

arrogance, an inflated opinion of one's own importance, power, and ability. It fosters the idea that we're self-sufficient and don't need anyone. And it works itself out in our vain attempts to seek glory and praise from others. At its deepest level, as Thomas Aquinas has said, the heart and soul of pride is "contempt for God and the refusal to obey Him."[3]

Sounds like our great enemy, Satan, doesn't it? That's because he is its originator. Pride is older than the Fall, reaching all the way back to another fall, this one involving God's highest created angelic being—Lucifer, the bright morning star. Read carefully Isaiah's brief but telling account of what happened.

> "How you have fallen from heaven,
> O star of the morning, son of the dawn!
> You have been cut down to the earth,
> You who have weakened the nations!
> But you said in your heart,
> 'I will ascend to heaven;
> I will raise my throne above the stars of God,
> And I will sit on the mount of assembly
> In the recesses of the north.
> I will ascend above the heights of the clouds;
> I will make myself like the Most High.'"
> (14:12–14)

Over the years, some have interpreted this passage as describing an unnamed Babylonian tyrant who took delight in mocking the Lord. But more conservative scholars agree that Isaiah is describing the dark event in past history when Lucifer swelled with pride and sought God's crown as the supreme sovereign ruler. Did you notice his five "I wills"? He wanted God's throne, His glory, and above all, he wanted to make himself "like the Most High."

Blinded with pride, Lucifer actually thought he could usurp the control of the universe from his Master. It was the height of arrogance; and from that pinnacle, he was "thrust down to Sheol, To the recesses of the pit" (v. 15). No longer the bright morning star, Lucifer instantly became Satan, the evil one, the prince of darkness.

He was given a kingdom to rule, but it wasn't what he had expected. It was hell, and he was its first inhabitant. Since that

---

3. Thomas Aquinas, as stated by Schimmel in *Seven Deadly Sins*, p. 25.

time he has sought to fill it with others who will make the same mistake he did and rebel against God out of pride. If you should doubt this, just go back and read how he tempted Eve in the Garden. Remember how he baited her with the puffed-up promise that if she ate the forbidden fruit she would become "like God" (Gen. 3:4–5)? Sound familiar? Exactly; he figured that what worked on him would work on her—and it did (v. 6).

What Is God's Opinion of It?

Even a cursory reading of the Bible will reveal that God reserves some of His strongest words of condemnation for this particular sin. In fact, whenever sins are listed in Scripture, pride is most often mentioned first. Here are just a few examples from the Old Testament.

> There are six things which the Lord hates,
> Yes, seven which are an abomination to Him:
> Haughty eyes, a lying tongue,
> And hands that shed innocent blood,
> A heart that devises wicked plans,
> Feet that run rapidly to evil,
> A false witness who utters lies,
> And one who spreads strife among brothers.
> (Prov. 6:16–19)

> "Pride and arrogance and the evil way,
> And the perverted mouth, I hate." (8:13b)

> Everyone who is proud in heart is an
>   abomination to the Lord;
> Assuredly, he will not be unpunished. . . .
> Pride goes before destruction,
> And a haughty spirit before stumbling.
> (16:5, 18)[4]

Switching over to the New Testament, the apostle Paul describes those whom God has given over to depraved minds as being

> filled with all unrighteousness, wickedness, greed, evil;
> full of envy, murder, strife, deceit, malice; they are
> gossips, slanderers, haters of God, *insolent, arrogant,*
> *boastful,* inventors of evil, disobedient to parents,

---

4. See also Proverbs 11:2a; 15:25; 21:4; 28:25; 29:23.

without understanding, untrustworthy, unloving, unmerciful. (Rom. 1:29–31, emphasis added)

"Arrogant" and "boastful" are also found in 2 Timothy 3, where Paul explains why difficult times will come in the last days.

For men will be lovers of self, lovers of money, boastful, arrogant, revilers, disobedient to parents, ungrateful, unholy, unloving, irreconcilable, malicious gossips, without self-control, brutal, haters of good, treacherous, reckless, conceited, lovers of pleasure rather than lovers of God; holding to a form of godliness, although they have denied its power. (vv. 2–5a)

One final reference which should make God's opinion perfectly clear is found in James 4.

"God is opposed to the proud, but gives grace to the humble." (v. 6b; see also 1 Pet. 5:5–6; 1 John 2:15–16)

Unequivocally, God opposes, God resists, God hates haughty looks, proud hearts, and arrogant spirits. Why so vehemently? Because, as Aquinas pointed out, more than any other sin, pride represents contempt for Him and the rebellious determination to disobey Him.

How Does Pride Manifest Itself?

Unlike gluttony, anger, and greed, which are often easily detected, pride can blend in to just about any lifestyle, making it practically impossible to detect. In our day, though, it seems that pride needn't bother to conceal itself because many people have exalted it from the vice that it is into a virtue it is not.

Some of the more obvious expressions of pride fanning its feathers are (1) an air of superiority, (2) an attitude of selfishness, (3) a win-at-any-cost determination where relationships are sacrificed on the altar of success, (4) a pursuit of praise at any price, and (5) a lust for public applause, commonly referred to as "playing to the grandstand."

Pride can also be subtle and deceptive, particularly in the way it uses things our culture is obsessed with, like physical attractiveness, wealth, knowledge, social status, and power over others. For example:

• putting others down through our claim to have "taste"

15

- being anxious that others know of our educational achievements or honors we've won

- holding ourselves aloof from those whose occupations are blue-collar, because the world says that highly paid professional jobs are more prestigious

Knowing that God hates this kind of arrogant attitude in all its manifestations, it should come as no surprise that there are occasions when He casts down prideful people just as He did Satan.

Is There a Particular Example in Scripture?

No one could testify to God's active hatred toward pride better than that king from ancient Babylon, Nebuchadnezzar. Centuries ago, Nebuchadnezzar ruled over one of the greatest empires in the history of civilization. He was brave, wealthy, brilliant, powerful, and popular . . . but he was also proud. When Daniel interpreted one of the king's dreams, he warned him to "break away now from your sins by doing righteousness," but he ignored him (Dan. 4:27). Twelve months later, Nebuchadnezzar was strutting around on the palace roof, boasting, "Is this not Babylon the great, which I myself have built . . . by the might of my power and for the glory of my majesty?" (v. 30), when God suddenly had enough of this proud peacock and changed him into a hideous beast.

> "While the word was in the king's mouth, a voice came from heaven, saying, 'King Nebuchadnezzar, to you it is declared: sovereignty has been removed from you, and you will be driven away from mankind, and your dwelling place will be with the beasts of the field. You will be given grass to eat like cattle, and seven periods of time will pass over you, until you recognize that the Most High is ruler over the realm of mankind, and bestows it on whomever He wishes.' Immediately the word concerning Nebuchadnezzar was fulfilled; and he was driven away from mankind and began eating grass like cattle, and his body was drenched with the dew of heaven, until his hair had grown like eagles' feathers and his nails like birds' claws." (vv. 31–33)

The humiliating misery of that animal-like existence got Nebuchadnezzar's attention. When it was over, he immediately boasted of God's sovereign power instead of his own.

> "I blessed the Most High and praised and honored
> Him who lives forever;
> > For His dominion is an everlasting
> > dominion,
> > And His kingdom endures from generation
> > to generation.
> > And all the inhabitants of the earth are
> > accounted as nothing,
> > But He does according to His will in the host
> > of heaven
> > And among the inhabitants of earth;
> > And no one can ward off His hand
> > Or say to Him, 'What hast Thou done?' . . .
> Now I Nebuchadnezzar praise, exalt, and honor the
> King of heaven, for all His works are true and His
> ways just, and He is able to humble those who walk
> in pride." (vv. 34b–35, 37)

Practical Warnings We Must Never Forget

It's not likely that God will send a prophet to warn us of our pride, but He has given us His Word to do the job instead. So let these three final thoughts from our study serve as a sobering caution concerning that most deadly of sins—pride.

First, *remember that God hates nothing like He hates pride*, whether it's overt or subtle, spoken or silent. Never forget that God is opposed to the proud (James 4:6a). Second, *remember that God humbles those who walk in pride* (Dan. 4:37). He is able to crush and cast down king or slave, educated or uneducated, influential or powerless, wealthy or poor. And third, *remember that God gives grace only to the humble* (James 4:6b). Do you want to be used by Him, to find His favor, to experience His blessing? Then humble yourself and praise, exalt, and honor the King of heaven just as Nebuchadnezzar did.

 Living Insights STUDY ONE

The kid really did look kind of, well, you know, dangerous. Baggy pants, skull-and-crossbones T-shirt, earring—definitely not your clean-cut, all-American, Disney World type. "Wanna buy some

T-shirts?" he pitched, holding up something I hardly glanced at.

"No," I said, waving him away without even giving my friends or family a chance to say anything. We were trying to enjoy a birthday meal together. Besides that, I was sick and tired of being bombarded by people wanting to sell me something. Half the phone calls I get anymore are people who mispronounce my last name and then ask me to buy something.

"But they're $24 in the store; I can give them to you for . . .

"NO!" I interrupted.

. . . just $12.95 apiece."

I shook my head disgustedly, like I was English nobility snubbing some scruffy street urchin. He caught that look, every bit of it, and backed away bidding us, me, to "Have a good day."

That's when I realized it. I heard it in his voice; the hurt that comes from being made to feel like you're a nobody, a loser—go away. I had been too quick to judge, too rude, too prideful. I've had people treat me that way before, and it's awful. I think that's why God hates arrogance so much. Because, in a way, that's what we say to Him with it, "You're a nobody, a loser—go away!"

Of course, I immediately got up and went over to apologize. Well, I thought about it. No, not even that, really. Actually, I just sat there eating my burger and making excuses for why I really didn't need to ask his forgiveness. "He doesn't care. . . . It wasn't really hurt that I sensed; it was something else. . . . He'll probably laugh in my face, and then I'll feel like a nobody, a loser—go away." Then, too, there was the teensy little problem of embarrassment. What will all these people around us think if they see nice-looking me apologizing to scuzzy-looking him?

He finally left, walking right past me while I just kept eating my hamburger. I know, I know, I blew it. As soon as we walked out into the parking lot, I paused and asked for Christ's forgiveness. But do you know what keeps haunting me? Jesus' words in Matthew 25, "Truly I say to you, to the extent that you did not do it to one of the least of these, you did not do it to Me" (v. 45). And what did I not do? Clothe that young boy with dignity, give him kindness to drink, or share even a morsel of compassion. Why? Because I was more concerned about my pride, the very thing God hates, than I was about the very things God loves, which are humility and that boy.

Who was that "least-of-all"-looking kid? Someone we all know. He's our neighbor, perhaps, or maybe a coworker or a member of our church. He's the prisoner, the widow, the destitute, and the sick. Who is it for you, and how are you treating him or her? Could it be that, like me, your pride is causing this other person to feel like a nobody, a loser? If so (be honest—I've told you about my dark side), what can you do now, today, to treat this person with the dignity you'd give to Christ?

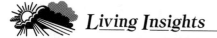 **Living Insights**

Many of us don't have that many feathers to fan when it comes to being prideful about our possessions. A couple of old cars, hand-me-down furniture, and the same old towels we received at our wedding shower pretty much tell the story. Nevertheless, pride can still creep into our attitudes. How? Well, we can become prideful over the fact that we're not materialistic. We can become proud of our "doing without." Don't laugh, it's true! . . . just like those Pharisees who used to love putting on their long, haggard faces so that everyone would know they were fasting and praise them for their spirituality (see Matt. 6:1–18). See how it works?

Is your Bible knowledge a source of pride, something you enjoy flaunting in front of others? Have your prayers ceased to be heartfelt communion with God and become rehearsed rituals designed to play to the crowd? Is your giving a source of pride?

Take a moment now to look for the presence of pride in the last place you would normally look—in your own personal practice of spiritual disciplines.

_____

_____

_____

_____

_____

_____

_____

_____

Chapter 3

LUST:
SEX OUT OF CONTROL
Selected Scriptures

In its broadest sense, lust means "to have an intense desire or need."[1] It could be for power, prestige, wealth, or even revenge, just to name a few. But for this particular study, our focus will center on that all-too-familiar craving explicitly paraded in films, magazines, on television, and over the airwaves—sexual immorality.

Now, before some of you jump to any conclusions, understand that we're not saying sex or sexual desire is sinful. As is obvious from Genesis 1 and 2, God not only created us male and female, He also brought the first man and woman together as husband and wife with the blessing, "Be fruitful and multiply" (1:28). Adam and Eve were free in the protective boundary of marital love to enjoy all the blessings of a close relationship, including intimate physical contact culminating with sexual intercourse (see also 4:1).

The Song of Solomon affirms this positive biblical view of sex by unabashedly extolling the physical delights of married love. In this passionate love song between a king and his bride, both revel in praising and caressing the other's body, giving us a healthy picture of intimate love as God intended it to be.

Hebrews 13:4 plants a protective hedge around a husband and a wife's sexual intimacy, warning: "Let the marriage bed be undefiled; for fornicators and adulterers God will judge" (v. 4b).

Fornication and adultery. These are but two examples of sex out of control, the difference between *intimate love*—the enjoyment of the gift of sex with one's marital partner; and *erotic lust*—improper, illicit, or unnatural expressions of sexual involvement.

Erotic Lust versus Intimate Love: There Is a Difference

Let's compare lust and love to further highlight their polar differences.

---

1. *Merriam-Webster's Collegiate Dictionary*, 10th ed., see "lust."

20

Erotic Lust	_Intimate Love_
1. Never fully satisfied. Leads to greater secrecy, hidden activities, and becomes a self-absorbed preoccupation. Feelings of alienation/self-hatred often follow the act.	1. Is regularly satisfied within the marriage relationship. Leads to greater openness, enjoyable creativity, and exists for the delight of one's partner. Intensified affection follows.
2. Is built on fantasies. As the drive takes over, unnatural and improper extremes become commonplace. Force may be present, where one sexually coerces the other. Leads to addiction.	2. Is based on reality. Honors the limits of human dignity and leads to a bond of closeness with one's partner. No force involved.
3. Results in painful and hurtful consequences. The longer lust takes charge, the greater the loneliness and more extensive the shame.	3. Results in increased pleasure and guilt-free relief as sexual drive is fulfilled. Other person never feels used or abused.

As for similarities, both erotic lust and intimate love arouse excitement as well as intense pleasure and physical satisfaction. If not controlled within biblical bounds, though, these powerful sensations can grab hold of our minds, whether we're married or not, and turn the blessing of sexual drive into a degrading addiction to unspeakable lusts.

A Brief but Pointed Scriptural Survey of Lust

Tucked away in the pages of Scripture are several real-life examples of those who became enslaved to lust.

In the Old Testament

Genesis 19 records the perversity of Sodom, an entire city dominated by homosexuality. So militantly depraved were its inhabitants that when two angels, appearing as men, visited Lot, the men of Sodom quickly surrounded Lot's house and demanded that he bring his visitors out so they could have sex with them.

Judges 16 bluntly tells of Samson's fall to the lust of fornication.

After twenty years as Israel's judge, Samson slipped away from his people and went in to a prostitute in an enemy city. From there he sought pleasure in the charms of Delilah. "His physical strength was unmatched," writes one commentator, "except by his moral weakness."[2]

Second Samuel 11 unfolds the story of David's adulterous liaison with Bathsheba. After enjoying a voyeuristic rooftop view of her bathing, the king immediately had her brought to his palace to satisfy his lust.

In the New Testament

Continuing our survey into the New Testament, we don't find as many personal accounts of sexual lust as we do strong admonitions against it. Consider the following:

- Homosexual relationships: "For this reason God gave them over to degrading passions; for their women exchanged the natural function for that which is unnatural, and in the same way also the men abandoned the natural function of the woman and burned in their desire toward one another, men with men committing indecent acts and receiving in their own persons the due penalty of their error" (Rom. 1:26–27).

- Incestuous relationships: "It is actually reported that there is immorality among you, and immorality of such a kind as does not exist even among the Gentiles, that someone has his father's wife. . . . I have decided to deliver such a one to Satan for the destruction of his flesh, that his spirit may be saved in the day of the Lord Jesus" (1 Cor. 5:1, 5; see also vv. 9–11).

- Illicit, immoral relations of any kind: "For this is the will of God, your sanctification; that is, that you abstain from sexual immorality; that each of you know how to possess his own vessel in sanctification and honor, not in lustful passion, like the Gentiles who do not know God; and that no man transgress and defraud his brother in the matter because the Lord is the avenger in all these things, just as we also told you before and solemnly warned you. For God has not called us for the purpose

---

2. F. Duane Lindsey, "Judges," in *The Bible Knowledge Commentary*, Old Testament edition, ed. John F. Walvoord and Roy B. Zuck (Wheaton, Ill.: Scripture Press Publications, Victor Books, 1985), p. 407.

of impurity, but in sanctification" (1 Thess. 4:3–7).

Two Cases of Lust in Contrast

Let's examine in detail two more Old Testament stories, one that illustrates lust out of control, and the other, lust kept under control.

Lust Revealed

Second Samuel 13 unfolds the sad details of an incestuous rape involving two of King David's children: Amnon, David's oldest son; and Tamar, Amnon's beautiful half sister.

According to verses 1–7, Amnon was infatuated with Tamar. His love, if it ever truly was that, became a burning lust that consumed him. With the help of a corrupt cousin named Jonadab, Amnon devised a plan to feign sickness so that Tamar could be requested to come to his home and care for him. She came, innocently unaware of the trap she was walking into.

> So Tamar went to her brother Amnon's house, and he was lying down. And she took dough, kneaded it, made cakes in his sight, and baked the cakes. And she took the pan and dished them out before him, but he refused to eat. And Amnon said, "Have everyone go out from me." So everyone went out from him. Then Amnon said to Tamar, "Bring the food into the bedroom, that I may eat from your hand." So Tamar took the cakes which she had made and brought them into the bedroom to her brother Amnon. When she brought them to him to eat, he took hold of her and said to her, "Come, lie with me, my sister." But she answered him, "No, my brother, do not violate me, for such a thing is not done in Israel; do not do this disgraceful thing! As for me, where could I get rid of my reproach? And as for you, you will be like one of the fools in Israel. Now therefore, please speak to the king, for he will not withhold me from you." However, he would not listen to her; since he was stronger than she, he violated her and lay with her. (vv. 8–14)

Our hearts break for Tamar, the helpless pleas, the fright, the physical violence, the shame. All because of lust—notice its familiar earmarks in this situation. Amnon became obsessed with his desire to the point of physical illness. The plot to entrap his sister was planned in secrecy. Deceit was employed to set up the situation. When Tamar refused his brash proposition, he, in turn, refused to listen to her pleas. Without remorse, Amnon raped her.

And afterward? Still another telltale sign of Amnon's lust surfaces to inflict even more pain on Tamar.

> Then Amnon hated her with a very great hatred; for the hatred with which he hated her was greater than the love with which he had loved her. And Amnon said to her, "Get up, go away!" But she said to him, "No, because this wrong in sending me away is greater than the other that you have done to me!" Yet he would not listen to her. Then he called his young man who attended him and said, "Now throw this woman out of my presence, and lock the door behind her." (vv. 15–17)

Though we have used restraint in describing this despicable act, do not turn away from it until the ugliness and violence impact you. Only then will you understand how sinister lust is. It will stop at nothing to gain satisfaction.

Lust Restrained

Now let's turn to a story in the life of Joseph where lust was restrained. This particular event occurred when Joseph was a slave in the household of an Egyptian officer named Potiphar (Gen. 39). Because the Lord was with Joseph and prospered all that he did, his master

> left everything he owned in Joseph's charge; . . . Now Joseph was handsome in form and appearance. (v. 6)

Did you notice that last part about his good looks? Potiphar's wife certainly did, and her lust impelled her to seduce him.

> And it came about after these events that his master's wife looked with desire at Joseph, and she said, "Lie with me." (v. 7)

Subtlety wasn't one of Mrs. Potiphar's strong suits, was it? Of

24

course, she didn't love Joseph, nor was she concerned about the consequences of her request. She wanted only one thing—her lust satisfied. But that's the one thing Joseph refused to give her.

> But he refused and said to his master's wife, "Behold, with me here, my master does not concern himself with anything in the house, and he has put all that he owns in my charge. There is no one greater in this house than I, and he has withheld nothing from me except you, because you are his wife. How then could I do this great evil, and sin against God?" (vv. 8–9)

Joseph's response reflects an incredible conscience and godly character. Surely Mrs. Potiphar felt ashamed of her bawdy behavior, apologized profusely, and never bothered him again, right? Wrong. She just kept right on trying to bait him.

> And it came about as she spoke to Joseph day after day, that he did not listen to her to lie beside her, or be with her. (v. 10)

Frustrated by his refusals, Mrs. Potiphar finally attempted to force Joseph to lie with her just as Amnon did with Tamar.

> Now it happened one day that he went into the house to do his work, and none of the men of the household was there inside. And she caught him by his garment, saying, "Lie with me!" And he left his garment in her hand and fled, and went outside. (vv. 11–12)

Fortunately, Joseph, unlike Tamar, had the strength to get physically free and flee. His is an incredible example of restraint which sends a clear message to us all that temptation can be conquered.

When the Sin of Lust Rears Its Ugly Head . . .

Such sterling examples as Joseph's are encouraging, but we need more than victorious testimonies to teach us how to effectively resist lust's alluring propositions. So let's close our study with these three practical measures each of us can employ.

First, *force yourself to focus on ultimate consequences when you're tempted by the immediate allurement.* Whether you're drawn to a pornographic film or magazine, the woman next to you at work, or the man two houses down, remember to always count the cost of your actions. What's done in secret will eventually be found out, and trouble will follow. You'll lose your self-respect, the peace within your heart, perhaps your family, your friend's trust, your career, even your health, to name only a few. Lust is only interested in being gratified *now*. To restrain it, you must force yourself to honestly face the consequences of the future.

Second, *train yourself to substitute new and wholesome alternatives to break old and unhealthy sexual habits.* Are you on the road a lot? Tell the hotel receptionist to block out all the pornographic TV channels before you go to your room. Do you have too much time on your hands that's being filled with steamy soap operas or erotic pulp novels? Develop an exercise program, sign up as a volunteer somewhere, or start a Scripture memory program with a friend. Have you already become addicted to pornography? Admit to yourself that you're a sexaholic and get help now! Face the problem. Let your pastor, a respected spiritual friend, or a counselor help you discover the different avenues of help available.

And third, *remind yourself that yielding this time will mean only greater difficulty saying no the next time.* Frederick Buechner wrote, "Lust is the craving for salt of a man who is dying of thirst."[3] Lust never satisfies; it only creates more thirst, driving its victims deeper into ever more desperate and degrading acts. It absolutely will not put on the brakes itself. You must.

 Living Insights STUDY ONE

> "You have heard that it was said, 'You shall not commit adultery'; but I say to you, that everyone who looks on a woman to lust for her has committed adultery with her already in his heart." (Matt. 5:27–28)

When it comes to lust, none of us are innocent, none of us can cast the first stone, not even at Amnon. So let's drop those stones of self-righteousness and come to grips with the real temptations troubling us, such as impure thoughts, pornography, and the host of other sexual sins lust can lure us into.

3. Frederick Buechner, *Wishful Thinking: A Theological ABC* (New York, N.Y.: Harper and Row, Publishers, 1973), p. 54.

Because of the sensitivity of this topic, we won't ask you to write out your thoughts in the guide, but you may want to write them on a scrap of paper to throw away after you've finished.

- Is there a particular lust gaining control in your life? Force yourself right now to focus on the ultimate consequences of this sin. What will you lose? What have you already lost? Think in terms of how this applies not only to you personally, but to your family, friends, church, career, Christian witness, and relationship with the Lord. Think hard about this. Don't minimize or rationalize the potential damage.

- Next, train yourself to substitute new, wholesome alternatives to break the old habits. Does a particular place, activity, or person trigger this lust's temptation? What wholesome substitutes could you pursue? Is there someone who can help hold you accountable? Are there some simple, practical precautions you could employ, like telling a hotel receptionist to block the porno channels on your TV?

- Finally, remind yourself that yielding this time will only make it more difficult to say no the next. C. S. Lewis once wrote:

> Every time you make a choice you are turning the central part of you, the part of you that chooses, into something a little different from what it was before. And taking your life as a whole, with all your innumerable choices, all your life long you are slowly turning this central thing either into a heavenly creature or into a hellish creature: either into a creature that is in harmony with God, and with other creatures, and with itself, or else into one that is in a state of war and hatred with God, and with its fellow-creatures, and with itself. To be the one kind of creature is heaven: that is, it is joy and peace and knowledge and power. To be the other means madness, horror, idiocy, rage, impotence, and eternal loneliness. Each of us at each moment is progressing to the one state or the other.[4]

4. C. S. Lewis, *Mere Christianity* (New York, N.Y.: Macmillan Publishing Co., 1952), pp. 86–87.

In what direction are the choices you make taking you? How deep has this lust left its mark on your soul already? Lewis continues,

> One man may be so placed that his anger sheds the blood of thousands, and another so placed that however angry he gets he will only be laughed at. But the little mark on the soul may be much the same in both. Each has done something to himself which, unless he repents, will make it harder for him to keep out of the rage next time he is tempted, and will make the rage worse when he does fall into it. Each of them, if he seriously turns to God, can have that twist in the central man straightened out again: each is, in the long run, doomed if he will not.[5]

Do you need to stop right now and ask God for the strength to say no to this particular lust? Remember God's promise to Paul, which is also intended for you, "My grace is sufficient for you, for power is perfected in weakness" (2 Cor. 12:9a).

Living Insights   STUDY TWO

Though we may like to believe that sexual immorality only happens to a few on the fringe, in reality, many in the mainstream also struggle in this area. If you are one of these secret strugglers, this Living Insight is for you.

———◆———

Sexual immorality, an addiction to pornography . . . how did it happen? When did it begin? Perhaps you can remember a specific time or event, perhaps not. The fact is, you're caught up in it and have not been able to break away. You've tried, really. But you keep going back to it and have been for years.

You're not some crazed-looking fiend, however. You haven't left your family or denied your faith. Quite the opposite. You've tried to grow, tried to lead a faithful and responsible life. And in the midst of all this, you have gradually taken on bigger and bigger responsibilities. Someone asked you to lead in worship, teach a Bible study, serve as a deaconess or elder, or pastor a church. Your

---

5. Lewis, *Mere Christianity*, p. 87.

first reaction was to say no. The guilt of your hidden sin was too much. It would be too hypocritical. But then you thought, "I'm going to quit. This is it, I'll stop." So you confessed the sin, asked for God's strength to stay pure, and took the position offered.

For a while you did stop, and it seemed that you had overcome the addiction; but then it started all over again—the sin, the lies, the covering up. You felt guilty and wanted to confess, but the terror of revealing this sin and facing all its horrible ramifications drove you to rationalize instead. "There's no need to bring it up, I'm going to quit. That's the last time I'll ever do that."

But of course, it wasn't. You're still addicted. And your life has become a living hell, a house divided against itself. You want to serve Christ, but you cannot escape the bondage to this other master. Now, today, years since this all began, you're wondering, "How can I confess this? Who will love me when I tell them I'm addicted to pornography or have been a child molester or have been involved in homosexuality? I'll lose everything—friends, family, position, privileges. What can I do?"

◆

There is no easy way to regain your integrity after living a lie for years. The truth is, it will be a painful process to expose this sinful part of your private life. But it's better to do what is right and suffer for it than to continue living a life of hypocrisy and deception. The one pain will lead to healing, the other only to deeper misery for you and many others.

If you're tired of carrying this tremendous burden, if you're sick of being a hypocrite and want to break free of this bondage, pray for God to guide you to someone whose spiritual maturity you respect. Perhaps a pastor or counselor—someone who has experience in helping broken people seek restoration. Then take a step of faith and confess your secret to this person. Will you take time to begin praying for God to show you whom this person might be?[6]

6. This Living Insight is adapted from the study guide *Christ at the Crossroads*, coauthored by Lee Hough, from the Bible-teaching ministry of Charles R. Swindoll (Anaheim, Calif.: Insight for Living, 1991), pp. 131–32.

Chapter 4

A CAREFUL ANALYSIS OF THE UNBORN

Psalm 139:13–18

The most dangerous place to be today is not on some distant battlefield dodging bullets and bombs. It's not in low-income, inner-city neighborhoods ruled by violent gangs. It's not even in the over-crowded prisons caging society's most unwanted. As life-threatening as these may be, they still cannot compare with that most dangerous of all places—the womb of a woman who doesn't want her unborn child.

Ironically, the very place traditionally revered as a haven of safety has become a killing chamber in a silent holocaust that efficiently destroys 4,383 babies a day.[1] Since 1973, when abortion became legal through *Roe v. Wade*, the abortion industry has taken the lives of more people than all the combat-related deaths in America since the Revolutionary War.

American War Casualties

Each cross mark represents 25,000 people killed. . . .

Revolutionary War	25,324	†
Civil War	498,332	†††††††††††††††††††††
World War I	116,708	†††††
World War II	407,316	†††††††††††††††
Korean War	54,246	††
Vietnam War	58,655	†††
War on the Unborn . . . since abortion was legalized in 1973	20,000,000	††††††††††††††††††††† ††††††††††††††††††††† ††††††††††††††††††††† †††††††††††††††††††††

††
††
††
††
††

1. Charles R. Swindoll, *Sanctity of Life* (Dallas, Tex.: Word Publishing, 1990), p. 13. Swindoll adds, "95-plus percent of children killed by abortion are killed for reasons of convenience; not incest, not rape, not the physical condition of the unborn, and not the threatened health of the mother" (p. 12).

†††
†††
†††
†††
†††
†††
†††
†††
†††
†††
†††
†††
†††
†††

"American War Casualties," used by permission of Right to Life of Greater Cincinnati.

Weep for all the little children, the would-be baseball players and ballerinas so brutally poisoned or dismembered. Their deaths, chillingly stacked like so much statistical cordwood, bring back haunting images of another Holocaust. Looking back, people often wonder with dumbfounded amazement at how educated and refined Germans could exterminate millions of people with such cool detachment. What was it that made such a colossal evil possible? In part, it was because the victims were not considered people. Their rights had been stripped away the same as today's unborn child. Reclassified as inferior, useless, and socially unwanted, they could be legally terminated simply because they did not serve the best interest of the Third Reich. In the same way, a woman today can terminate the life of her unborn child simply because it is "not in her best interest" to bear it.

That's what makes the womb of a woman who doesn't want her baby the most dangerous place to be. Pro-abortionists have fostered new laws declaring that the developing baby is not a living person but just insensible fetal tissue. If that's true—that the fetus is not human life with all its attendant rights—then a woman's decision to have it terminated is no more a moral decision than if she were having a tumor removed.

But if it is life?

The core issue of the abortion controversy has to do with that four-letter word, *L-I-F-E*. Who will decide the unborn's status? Who should? Attorneys? Activists? Physicians? Politicians? Though each of these may provide expert opinions, God's opinion transcends them all to give us absolute truth concerning the unborn. He alone, as Creator, has the right to settle the issue of when life begins. So let's carefully examine His perspective, as expressed by David in Psalm 139.

Biblical Insights from the Inspired Psalmist

Psalm 139 is actually an ancient hymn composed of four stanzas with six verses in each. David wrote it as a prayer, and in its first three stanzas he meditatively reflects on different characteristics of God. This context is important to remember because it provides the background for the verses we'll study in detail.

The first stanza, then, in verses 1–6, reveals God's *omniscience*— "My Maker knows everything!" The second stanza, verses 7–12, describes His *omnipresence*—"My Maker is everywhere!" And third, in verses 13–18, the focus is on God's *omnipotence*—"My Maker is in control of every part of life!"

In this third stanza, David's thoughts, like a fiber-optic probe in the hands of the Holy Spirit, take us into the dark world of a mother's womb to reveal some of its innermost secrets. As we examine each of his observations closely, paying special attention to the various meanings of the original Hebrew words, we will find the answer to our question dealing with the unborn—is it life?

Verse 13

For Thou didst form my inward parts;
Thou didst weave me in my mother's womb.

David opens this verse using an emphatic Hebrew term for the word "Thou," which, given its proper emphasis, would translate into something like this: *"You, Yourself, Lord—acting alone and without the assistance of another—only You* formed my inward parts."

Who brings about the miracle of conception? A man and woman having intercourse? Mother Nature? No! Conception is not merely a biological process nor is it controlled by some mythological person. God is the One who forms, meaning "originates," our existence in the womb. His sovereignty extends even to the microscopic realm of the sperm and the egg to superintend the creation of life through fertilization.

Two more insights come to light as we look through the lens of David's inspired word for *inward parts*. First, the Hebrew term literally means "kidneys," which, in that day, referred to all the vital organs such as the heart, brain, lungs, and liver. And as German scholar Dr. Franz Delitzsch further observes, it also refers to "the seat of the tenderest, most secret emotions."[2] So, along with our internal organs, the Father oversees the development of our inner selves, the intangible longings and desires of our hearts.

Still another word vividly describing God's delicate work is found in the second half of verse 13: "Thou didst weave me in my mother's womb." The term for *weave* means "to plait, interweave, . . . with bones, sinews, and veins."[3] From a single cell to a fully developed baby, the material parts of our anatomy are lovingly knitted together by an invisible Weaver.

Putting together all that we've discovered thus far, a loose translation of verse 13 might read, "For You, Lord (and no other), originated my vital organs—including even my emotional makeup. You knitted together my bones, muscles, and veins while I was in my mother's womb."

Verse 14

Struck with amazed fascination at how wonderfully God had made him, David breaks forth in spontaneous praise:

> I will give thanks to Thee, for I am fearfully and
>   wonderfully made;
> Wonderful are Thy works,
> And my soul knows it very well.

It thrilled the author's soul to consider the minute details of God's handiwork in the workshop of the womb. He exulted in the mystery of something he couldn't fully explain but could readily accept.

Verse 15

Refocusing his thoughts on the womb, David continues,

> My frame was not hidden from Thee,
> When I was made in secret,
> And skillfully wrought in the depths of the earth.

By *frame* David is referring to the skeleton, because the term

---

2. Franz Delitzsch, *The Psalms*, vol. 3 of 3 vols. in 1, in *Commentary on the Old Testament in Ten Volumes*, by C. F. Keil and F. Delitzsch (reprint; Grand Rapids, Mich.: William B. Eerdmans Publishing Co., 1978), vol. 5, p. 349.

3. Delitzsch, *The Psalms*, p. 349. See also Roy B. Zuck, "Job," in *The Bible Knowledge Commentary*, Old Testament ed., ed. John F. Walvoord and Roy B. Zuck (Wheaton, Ill.: Scripture Press Publications, Victor Books, 1985), p. 732.

actually means "bony substance." God not only knits our vital organs and tender emotions together, He also constructs the sturdy orthopedic frame to support them.

All this embryonic building takes place "in secret," within the invisible walls of the uterus. Poetically described as "the depths of the earth,"[4] David says it was in that divinely designed shelter that he was "skillfully wrought." Some of you who do needlework will especially appreciate the term David chose to communicate this, which means "embroidered." The multiple thousands of veins and arteries that run through the body in a colorful network are like variegated threads worked into a piece of tapestry by the patient hands of One who is a skilled artist.

Once again, let's pause to paraphrase our findings. "My skeleton, which determines my height, shape, posture, and size, was not hidden from You, Lord, when You made me in that secret, protected place—the place where You artistically weaved together my veins, arteries, and entire internal system like fine needlepoint."

Verse 16

The remarkable truth expressed in this next verse removes all doubts that any conception is an "accident" or a surprise to the Lord.

> Thine eyes have seen my unformed substance;
> And in Thy book they were all written,
> The days that were ordained for me,
> When as yet there was not one of them.

God knew David even before he was conceived in his mother's womb. All his days, from the moment of conception to his last breath, had already been arranged by the Lord before the shepherd boy and king lived even one of them. From start to finish, it is not we who are in charge, but the Lord. It is not we who give life, but God.

Overcome by God's thoughts toward him, David reciprocates, saying,

> How precious also are Thy thoughts to me, O God!
> How vast is the sum of them!
> If I should count them, they would outnumber
> the sand.

---

4. In ancient times, priceless treasures were often buried or tucked away in a dark place, protected from peering eyes. In the same way, God's embryonic treasure is sequestered until His masterpiece is complete.

When I awake, I am still with Thee. (vv. 17–18)

As a way of concluding our time with David, let's again rephrase his thoughts for a final glimpse into the mysteries surrounding life as it begins in the womb.

"Your eyes watched over me when I was just an embryo; and in Your book the days I should experience were all described and recorded—the kind of days that would shape me into the person You wanted me to be—even before I was born. How priceless and mighty and vast and numerous are Your thoughts of me, O God. Should I attempt to count them, they would be more than the sand of the seashore. And Your plan isn't limited just to this life on earth. Should I die, I would awaken securely in Your arms; I would be with You more than ever before."

Practical Thoughts for All Expectant Parents

There are many things you won't hear in an abortion clinic. The fragile cries of newborn life. The tender coos of an exhausted but euphoric mother. The excited joy of a first-time father. The congratulations of doctors, nurses, and grinning grandparents. The proud calls to friends and relatives.

You also won't hear the three following statements that might have saved the lives of the 183 babies that will be aborted in about the time it takes to read these words.

First, *since you did not originate the life of your unborn, you have no right to end it.* Though our laws currently permit abortion, it is clear in the higher law of God's Word that the fetus in the womb is life, planned and ordained by Him.

Second, *since you do not know the plan God has for your unborn child, you need to allow that plan to take place.* Who are we to say what a child's future will be? If anything, history has shown that the greatest good often comes from where we least expect it.

Third, *since you cannot imagine the purposes God has for you regarding this baby, you must not interfere with what God has arranged.* While almost two million women a year are taking the lives of their babies, this is your opportunity to preserve your child's. This is your moment to affirm a living faith in the future God has planned for you and your baby.[5]

5. Abortion is an issue of such scope that we cannot address all the questions and concerns raised by this lesson. For further study, see "Books for Probing Further" at the end of the guide.

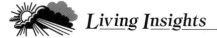

Let's continue examining the evidence as to the unborn being life by calling to the witness stand Dr. Norman Geisler.

Dr. Geisler, could you sum up in your own words the central issue at stake in this chapter?

"Whatever dispute there may be over which moral actions are prohibited by natural moral law, there is no dispute about one—the common value of protecting human life. All agree that we should never intentionally take the life of an innocent human being. If this is so, then there is only one relevant question when it comes to abortion—are unborn babies human beings? If they are human, then abortion is morally wrong. Not simply because the church or the Bible says it is wrong but because a moral law written on the heart of every human being says so."

Thank you. Now, Dr. Geisler, aside from any biblical evidences, some of which we've just examined in Psalm 139, are there any scientific facts that shed light on the life of the unborn?

"Modern science has provided a window on the womb. As a result, the evidence is now clearer than ever that individual human life begins at the very moment of conception (fertilization)."

For example?

"It is a genetic fact that a fertilized human ovum is 100 percent human. First of all, from that very moment all genetic information is present. No new information is added from the point of conception till death. Second, all physical characteristics for life are contained in that genetic code present at conception. Third, the sex of the individual child is determined at the moment of conception. Fourth, a female ovum has only 23 chromosomes. A male sperm has 23 chromosomes. A normal adult human being has 46 chromosomes. But at the very moment of conception, when the male sperm and the female ovum unite, a new tiny 46-chromosome human being emerges. Fifth, from the moment of conception till death nothing is added except food, air, and water."

In light of such facts, has the scientific community drawn any conclusions concerning the life of the unborn?

"On April 23, 1981, scientific experts from around the world testified as to the beginning of an individual life. Here is a summary of what was said:

- "In biology and in medicine, it is an accepted fact that the life of any individual organism resulting from sexual reproduction begins at conception, or fertilization. (Dr. Micheline M. Matthew-Ruth of Harvard University supported this from over 20 embryology and other scientific tests.)

- "To accept the fact that after fertilization has taken place a new human has come into being is no longer a matter of taste or opinion. The human nature of the human being from conception to old age is not a metaphysical contention, it is plain experimental evidence (world famous French geneticist Jerome LeJeune).

- "But now we can say, unequivocally, that the question of when life begins is no longer a question for theological or philosophical dispute. It is an established scientific fact. Theologians and philosophers may go on to debate the meaning of life or the purpose of life, but it is an established fact that all life, including human life, begins at the moment of conception (Dr. Hymie Gordon)."

Is there any other scientific evidence you would like to present to the court at this time?

"Modern fetology has brought to light some amazing things about the growth of this tiny person in his/her mother's womb which fetologists call their second 'patient.' The . . . vivid testimony to the full humanness of the prenatal child . . . make the identity of human embryos unmistakable. They are not mineral, vegetable, or animal; they are human. Since the factual evidence is overwhelmingly in favor of a new individual human life beginning at conception (fertilization), and since intentionally taking an innocent human life is morally wrong, it follows rationally and necessarily that abortion is morally wrong. . . . Abortion is not a religious issue; it is a human issue. It takes human lives."[6]

Thank you, Dr. Geisler, you may step down. Defense asks that a short recess be given so the reader has time to ponder these facts before beginning our second Living Insight.

6. Norman L. Geisler, "The Natural Right," in *In Search of a National Morality* (Grand Rapids, Mich.: Baker Book House; San Francisco, Calif.: Ignatius Press, 1992), pp. 119–22. Used by permission.

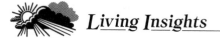

With the reader's permission, we'd like to recall Dr. Geisler to the witness stand.

Dr. Geisler, would you comment on the major arguments used to justify abortion?

"First, there is a woman's right over her own body. Second, there are situations in which the baby will be born hopelessly deformed. Third, there is the need to alleviate the insufferable indignity forced upon a woman by a pregnancy resulting from rape. Fourth, there are those unwanted pregnancies that make the child vulnerable to neglect and abuse. Fifth, why should a woman be forced against her will to bring into this world a baby she does not want? Finally, there is a need for compassion for the many women whose lives would be threatened by illegal abortion in back alleys with rusty coat hangers."

Sounds pretty persuasive.

"They are persuasive—granting one major assumption that the Supreme Court made when it legalized abortion on demand— namely, that the unborn being is not a human person protected by the Constitution but only a 'potential [human] life.' If the unborn is not an individual human being, then not only are these arguments good, they are even convincing."

So we're back to that crucial issue of whether the unborn are living human beings or not. If they are, as the Scriptures and science prove, then none of these arguments can justify taking their lives. True, these difficult dilemmas deserve to be addressed, but killing innocent human life is not the solution. Are there any other widely used arguments?

"There are always the more evasive intellects—often trained in philosophy—who insist on making distinctions not grounded in reality. For example, some argue that an unborn baby may be human but it is not a *person*. In response, several things should be noted. First, the argument is *philosophically arbitrary*. It has no essential grounds by which it makes this distinction, only accidental ones (such as size, shape, and location). Second, this distinction is *morally irrelevant*. The moral duty is to protect human life, not just persons. Third, it is *legally misdirected*. Corporations and even baby eagles are protected by our laws—how much more should unborn humans be protected! Fourth, it is *socially disastrous* since by the same reasoning one could declare all small children and adults who lack

38

certain functions to be 'nonpersons.' Fifth, it makes the question of when life begins *objectively indeterminable* since there is no other observable point at which to place the inception of life. Sixth, it leads to a moral absurdity, such as declaring that personhood begins at self-consciousness. But this would justify infanticide up to nearly two years after birth, the point at which self-consciousness is attained. . . .

"There is a second fallacy in all the 'good' arguments for abortion. As the late Princeton ethicist Professor Paul Ramsey warned, the same 'good' reasons put forward in defense of abortion are equally 'good' arguments for infanticide and euthanasia. In short, if we can kill babies before they are born because they are deformed, socially inconvenient, undesired, etc., then there is no ethical reason we cannot kill two-year-olds—or eighty-two-year-olds—on the same grounds."[7]

Thank you, Dr. Geisler. The witness is excused.

Our closing argument comes from a debate between pro-life activist Joseph Foreman and Barbara Radford of the National Abortion Federation.

> At one point in their exchange on CNN's "Crossfire," when the assault conviction of New York abortionist Abu Hayat was brought up, Foreman pounced. Earlier, Ms. Radford had expressed her disapproval of Hayat's botched third trimester abortion, which resulted in the shearing of an unborn girl's right arm but not her death. FOREMAN: ". . . You said you were horrified by the little girl who got her arm ripped off. . . ." MS. RADFORD: "I was." FOREMAN: "Would you not have been horrified if he could have ripped the other arm off, the leg off, crushed the skull, and finished the job so there would be no mess?" MS. RADFORD: "No, uh, that's not what we're here to talk about today. . . ."[8]

Oh, yes, it is. Defense rests.

---

7. Geisler, "The Natural Right," pp. 124–26. Used by permission.
8. "Inter Alia, Inter Alios," *World*, March 20–27, 1993, p. 8.

Chapter 5

IN DEFENSE OF THE HELPLESS

Selected Scriptures

Day and night they do not cease to say,
"Holy, holy, holy,
is the Lord God, the Almighty,
who was and who is and who is to come." (Rev. 4:8b)

The divine creatures surrounding God's throne continually reso-nate praise for His radiant purity. It is a natural outpouring, a consuming passion inspired by the splendor of His perfection. He is holy, wholly good, infinitely separated from all that's unholy.

In stark contrast, sin is ugly, ugly, ugly. Or, as F. B. Meyer once said, "Sin is dark, dangerous, damnable."[1] It is *dark* because evil hides in the shadows of a person's life. It seeks secrecy. It runs from exposure, deceives to stay undetected, and always despises the light of the truth.

Sin is *dangerous* because it hurts—both the sinner and the one sinned against. It also scars, steals innocence, and creates addictive inner torturings.

And sin is *damnable* because it deserves condemnation. It brings a curse upon a life, ruins reputations, and destroys the good effect of a lifetime of faithful service. Solomon underscored the damnable, self-made horror of sin:

> His own iniquities will capture the wicked,
> And he will be held with the cords of his sin.
> (Prov. 5:22; see also 6:32–33)

Now, since God is holy, holy, holy, and because sin is dark, dangerous, and damnable . . . Christ came. The Father sent His only Son to liberate us from our bondage to sin and death. "He made [Jesus] who knew no sin to be sin on our behalf, that we might become the righteousness of God in Him" (2 Cor. 5:21).

---

1. F. B. Meyer, *David: Shepherd, Psalmist, King* (Fort Washington, Pa.: Christian Literature Crusade, 1977), p. 199.

Only the redeemed, those who trust in Christ and are clothed with His righteousness, possess eternal life and the power to overcome sin.

Yet even though Jesus has made us alive to serve a holy God, Christians can live as if still enslaved to sin. And many do. A spiritual malaise of mediocrity and compromise has gripped the Church so tightly that it appears we have forgotten one of the oldest commands in all of Scripture—to be holy because God is holy.

Redeemed people are to have a lifestyle that reflects God's holy character. Nowhere is this more clearly spelled out than in Leviticus, Israel's handbook of life.

> "'I am the Lord your God. Consecrate yourselves therefore, and be holy; for I am holy.'" (11:44a)

Moses is instructed to repeat this same message in chapter 19, verse 2.

> "Speak to all the congregation of the sons of Israel and say to them, 'You shall be holy, for I the Lord your God am holy.'"

Now look at 20:7 and 26.

> "'You shall consecrate yourselves therefore and be holy, for I am the Lord your God. . . . Thus you are to be holy to Me, for I the Lord am holy; and I have set you apart from the peoples to be Mine.'"

Sandwiched between these last two verses, which stand like sacred bookends, are the most explicit laws concerning sexual morality in Scripture. For example:

> "'If there is a man who commits adultery with another man's wife, one who commits adultery with his friend's wife, the adulterer and the adulteress shall surely be put to death. If there is a man who lies with his father's wife, he has uncovered his father's nakedness; both of them shall surely be put to death, their bloodguiltiness is upon them. If there is a man who lies with his daughter-in-law, both of them shall surely be put to death; they have committed incest, their bloodguiltiness is upon them. If there is a man who lies with a male as those who lie with a woman, both of them have committed a

detestable act; they shall surely be put to death. Their bloodguiltiness is upon them. If there is a man who marries a woman and her mother, it is immorality; both he and they shall be burned with fire, that there may be no immorality in your midst. If there is a man who lies with an animal, he shall surely be put to death; you shall also kill the animal. If there is a woman who approaches any animal to mate with it, you shall kill the woman and the animal; they shall surely be put to death. Their bloodguiltiness is upon them.

'If there is a man who takes his sister, his father's daughter or his mother's daughter, so that he sees her nakedness and she sees his nakedness, it is a disgrace; and they shall be cut off in the sight of the sons of their people. He has uncovered his sister's nakedness; he bears his guilt.'" (vv. 10–17; see also 18:6–23)

Why such a detailed description of the deviant sexual behavior forbidden by God? Because Israel was to be separate, distinct from the pagan nations in the Promised Land where such practices were excused, overlooked, joked about, and enjoyed.

Those same practices of adultery, incest, fornication, bestiality, and homosexuality continue today, as does the Christian's call to reflect God's holiness in every aspect of his or her character. Peter reminds us of this in the New Testament, writing, "Like the Holy One who called you, be holy yourselves also in all your behavior" (1 Pet. 1:15). John adds, ". . . walk in the light as He Himself is in the light" (1 John 1:7). And Paul warns, ". . . be fearful of sinning" (1 Tim. 5:20).

But sin's dark cloud and dangerous grip and damnable impact have taken a terrible toll on our times. Much of what currently passes for Christianity does not reflect a healthy fear of God. His holiness and hatred of sin no longer influence the way many believers live. Instead of steering clear of sin, we now tolerate and flirt with it. Instead of running from evil, keeping ourselves at a safe distance from it, avoiding even the appearance of it, we casually allow it to coexist with godliness in our lives.

Stop and think about it. There once was a time when our culture

• considered the Christian's word his or her bond,

- expected the Christian's speech and motives to be pure,
- believed the Christian's integrity was intact,
- viewed the Christian's home as a place of safety where children grew up innocently, protected from the violence and shameful practices of the world,
- regarded the Christian's place of worship as a bulwark of truth and trusted leadership.

And how are Christians viewed today?

- We are no longer trusted by the public.
- We have lost the people's respect.
- We have lost our purity. Adultery, fornication, incest, homosexuality, pornography, molestation—the Church is overrun with lay-people and leaders alike who are bound by the cords of these sins.
- We have violated the safety of our homes with rampant divorce and every kind of abuse.

How terribly dark sin has become. God's commands to abstain from sexual immorality no longer bind many believers. Not even the threat of AIDS has slowed our philandering. All that matters now is practicing "safe sex."

How terribly dangerous sin has become. With our consciences dulled and our standards lowered, grievous sins go unnoticed. More than that, some are applauded and given special status, such as the ordination of practicing homosexuals. Jeremiah's words come back to haunt us:

> Were they ashamed because of the abomination
>   they have done?
> They were not even ashamed at all;
> They did not even know how to blush.
> (Jer. 6:15a)

How terribly damnable sin has become. To find immediate gratification, many so-called believers in Christ have gone to every extreme—seeking sex from whatever partner, in whatever manner, for whatever reason, at whatever expense, regardless of whatever consequences. And the ultimate tragedy is that innocent children, those who most deserve to be protected, have become fair game.

Tragically, the specter of pedophiles within the Church is a well-publicized reality. Much to our shame, molestation and incest in the homes of Christians are no longer a shock. Children, who have never been safe in the world, are now at risk even in the homes of some preachers and teachers![2]

What a sad, dark, dangerous, damnable day it is. And it only grows worse each time the Church covers up such heinous sins by refusing to expose the abusers and by not believing the victims.

The time has come, to borrow a phrase from the apostle Peter, "for judgment to begin with the household of God" (1 Pet. 4:17)! Is this not what Paul urged upon the church at Corinth? One of its members was openly committing incest, and instead of disciplining the man, the Corinthians boasted about their broad-minded acceptance of his behavior. "Remove the wicked man from among yourselves," Paul commanded (1 Cor. 5:13). Expose the sin, put an end to it, now.

Yet in our zeal to expose sin and restore holiness, let us not forget the victims. Remember not to treat them as Absalom did Tamar after he discovered she had been raped by her half brother, Amnon (2 Sam. 13:1–19). Look closely at his foolish counsel:

> "But now keep silent, my sister, he is your brother;
> do not take this matter to heart." (v. 20)

First, he tells Tamar to keep quiet, to pretend nothing ever happened by stuffing her hurt and shame deep within herself. Next, he reminds her that Amnon is family—she must loyally preserve the family's good name by keeping this ugly sin hidden. Last, he trivializes her trauma by telling her that what happened wasn't really all that bad. "Don't let it bother you," he says.

Absalom's advice couldn't have been more bitterly devastating for Tamar. She desperately needed to tell someone, to have an advocate recognize her pain, declare her innocence, and demand justice. Her father, David, should have been that person. We're told in verse 21 that he somehow heard of Tamar's rape and "was very angry." But as we read on in verse 23, we see that two years passed and he never did or said anything to address the wrong or help the

---

2. "At one time, sexual abuse was thought to occur most often between total strangers. . . . Now the grim facts are acknowledged: over eighty-five per cent of sexual abuse is committed by someone the child knows, loves and trusts." Alice Huskey, *Stolen Childhood: What You Need to Know about Sexual Abuse* (Downers Grove, Ill.: InterVarsity Press, 1990), p. 30.

victim, his own daughter. What a tragedy.

Remember, this all occurred when Tamar was a young woman. Can you imagine the confusion and the damage that occur when this same thing happens to a child? Sexually abused children know about the ugliness of sin. They learn about it early in life. It is their secret burden, something that strips away the joy and innocence of their childhood. For them the boogeyman is not a coat in the closet; it is a parent, relative, neighbor, perhaps even a trusted Christian leader whose closeted touch is dark, dangerous, damnable.

Yes, it is time for judgment to begin in the house of God. It is time for repentance and revival, because God has called us, His Church, to provide life-giving help—especially where children are concerned. So we must take a stand in at least three ways.

First, *since the world has never been a safe and secure place for children, the Church must be both.* It must be a shelter in the time of a child's storm, a place that can handle their secrets, a source of compassion for those who have been violated, molested, and abused.

Second, *since the home is no longer a harbor for the hurting, the Church must be the one place that can be trusted.*

- If you are being abused, you should be able to trust Christians to help.

- If you are being victimized, you should be able to tell your secret and be believed.

- If you are afraid, unsure, and in need of information, Christians ought to be equipped to give or direct you to professional assistance.

Third, *since the Church is the only place of refuge and relief for many, we must maintain an uncompromising commitment to holiness.* In plain terms, that means the Church should be neither passive nor tolerant toward anyone who would prey on the defenseless and the innocent. And toward believers who are victims, it means we shall be neither uncaring nor judgmental. As the body of Christ, we need to help victims, believe in them, step in and assist them in every way we can.

◆

When he delivered this message, Chuck Swindoll began it by saying, "'Sin is dark, dangerous, damnable.' I have become more aware of that this week than ever before in thirty years of ministry."

Here, in his own words, is the reason why.

"For the past number of days, several of us on the pastoral staff and elder board have been overwhelmed by grief and torn by disappointment upon hearing of the actions of one of our trusted leaders. As a result of tedious investigation and private examination, all of it handled discreetly and carefully, this person has been confronted and has admitted to a past life of hidden sin and has submitted his resignation from the Board of Elders of our church. This resignation has been heard by our Elder Board and General Board and accepted with great disappointment. I have been asked to read it to the congregation. I do so, believing that our church should be informed and made aware of this tragic confession with its widespread implications."

The elder's resignation was then read, in which he penitently confessed to a long history of molesting young girls.

Because the sin was of a scandalous nature, occurring over a long period of time and involving a number of girls—most of whom are now married with families—and because this individual held one of the highest offices within the church, the Board of Elders felt it was appropriate by unanimous decision to announce the resignation with the person's name attached (see 1 Tim. 5:20). And Chuck tearfully added, "I do so with a broken heart. I do not do this to hurt a man I have loved for twenty-one years. I do it to help heal the young women, some of whom we may not have even met yet."

Following this, Chuck read the formal steps of church discipline to be taken against both the elder and his wife.[3]

> It is with great sorrow yet with strong scriptural confidence that we relate to you the following decision of the Elder Board:
>
> A formal motion was made, seconded, and passed unanimously that:
>
> 1. The husband and wife's church membership shall be revoked.

---

3. It was felt that the wife was also culpable because she was aware of his problem with molestation but had kept this dark sin hidden with her silence and had not provided protection for the young girls who had innocently spent the night in their home. We are not publishing the couple's names because that is neither warranted nor appropriate.

46

2. Both shall be forbidden to be on church grounds at any time. Chuck explained, "We feel that is essential for the safety and relief of the victims. The only exception would be when they come for a confrontation session with families and victims."

3. Both shall remain accountable for a periodic review with members of the Elder Board of this church.

4. The husband will immediately inform the leadership of any other church he and his wife shall attend in the future concerning his past private lifestyle if he is asked to serve or lead in any manner.

Regarding the fourth point, the Elder Board stipulated that if he did not inform said church leaders, the elders at First Evangelical Free Church of Fullerton would be under obligation to do so.

Since both were teaching in an elementary Sunday school class, and knowing that this horrible news would especially alarm parents of young girls in the congregation, Chuck immediately quelled some fears by informing everyone that they had not found one case where the molestation had occurred on or around the church property. Thank God.

As he had said earlier in his message, the Church must be a safe harbor from sin, a trusted place that maintains an uncompromising commitment to holiness. And with that in mind, Chuck sent an emphatic message to any others within that congregation who might take inappropriate advantage of an innocent child.

This church will not tolerate this! This is not a place, though we are large, where you can hide! And children will be safe in this place! Because God is holy!

Finally, with the abuse and the abuser exposed, the discipline set, and a warning given, the pastor moved out of his role as protector and took up the servant's mantle as healer. The flock he shepherds had been severely wounded, some members more than others, and he needed to help them find still waters to restore their souls.

Chuck's first concern was to reassure any victims, whether or not they were victims of this particular perpetrator, that he was committed to keeping the church a safe place where they could come and find help. Having done that, he then asked the staff and elders, along with their mates, to stand before the congregation and be available to any who needed to talk further. Some would want to know more details, he realized, and if it was appropriate, they certainly would be given that information.

Second, for those who had been victimized by this man, as well as anyone needing help in dealing with this tragedy, a qualified counseling team was ready to offer assistance. They could expect trained, thorough, and confidential help.

And third, any parents wondering if their child was in this man's circle of abuse could meet with professional counselors and psychologists trained in helping detect whether a child had been abused and in what to do about it.

Our hope is that your church will never have to experience anything like this, but the dark, dangerous, damnable truth of sin in our day is that it very possibly could. Let's not stick our heads in the sand and pretend otherwise. For that reason, we have shared this difficult story. We hope that it might serve, in some small way, as a helpful pattern for exposing abusers and helping the victims.

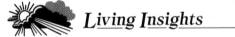 *Living Insights*

Many of us would like to think that child molesters live only in slums, crawling out at night like cockroaches to move among society's outcasts. We tend to caricature perpetrators of incest as uneducated degenerates who spend all their time scurrying to and from porno theaters and adult bookstores. We stubbornly cling to the belief that nice-looking church members are somehow immune from such filthy practices.

But these are only myths, which Lynn Heitritter and Jeanette Vought expose in their book *Helping Victims of Sexual Abuse*. Reflecting on one young girl's story of parental incest, they write, "Julie's father was not some sort of freakish pervert. Like many men who abuse their children, he was a well-respected, wealthy member of his community, and, in this case, a deacon in his church as well."[4]

4. Lynn Heitritter and Jeanette Vought, *Helping Victims of Sexual Abuse* (Minneapolis, Minn.: Bethany House Publishers, 1989), p. 15. Used by permission.

Try to understand. Sexual abuse knows no boundaries. It thrives today in every social, ethnic, and economic strata of our society. The statistics are staggering, and researchers generally agree that we're only seeing the tip of the iceberg. "Some sources indicate that every two minutes in the United States a child is sexually abused, but that less than 2% of molestations are ever reported."[5]

One of the reasons so few are reported, especially among young children, is because the signs of sexual abuse are often overlooked by those closest to the child. A key to early detection, Heitritter and Vought explain, is noticing a cluster of symptoms such as the ones described in their book.

Physical Signals

Some of the more overt physical signs of sexual abuse in a young child might be venereal disease, vaginitis, bladder infections, or pain in urinating or defecating. . . .

Persistent sore throats or unexplained gagging can be a symptom of abuse, due to the high incidence of forced oral sex, especially with younger children.

Behavioral Signals

Many behavioral changes may signal the onset of abuse. A young child may have appetite changes or some changes in sleeping patterns. Nightmares can be a sign of abuse, as well as a sudden onset of fears or anxieties.

Fear

A child may fear strange men or strange situations. . . . One young woman aged 25 told of being molested by her godfather when she was 8 years old. Thereafter, every time her parents wanted to go visit the godfather, who was a close friend of the family, she threw a temper tantrum and refused to go. . . . Fears of playing alone, unprovoked crying spells or regression in one or more developmental areas, such as bed-wetting, thumb-sucking, or

---

5. Heitritter and Vought, *Helping Victims of Sexual Abuse*, p. 13. Used by permission.

baby talk, can indicate the kinds of fears and stress experienced by an abused child.

Refusals

When a child resists a previously favorite activity, or refuses to be with a previously favorite person, the reason for that change should be carefully examined. . . .

Self-Injury/Graphic Play

Sometimes a child acts out the stress of the abuse by self-injurious behaviors such as biting themselves or others, cutting themselves, or by destructive, continuous masturbation. Perhaps a child will reveal the trauma of abuse by drawing pictures of adults' or children's genitals, especially with details like pubic hair.

Feeling "Bad"

A child betrayed by a trusted person has received the message that he or she is a "bad" child. Such children often feel tremendous guilt and shame in conflict with any positive feelings they may have for the offender. In order to shroud the secret, this conflict must be hidden as well. This may make it necessary for the child to move from the point of always "pretending" everything is OK to the point of becoming a skillful liar. . . .

Loss of Personal Identity

Sexual abuse is a violation of personal boundaries and confuses the child about his identity and his body. Some children may avoid all physical contact with others and refuse to be held, hugged, or cuddled. Others may appear listless, detached, or isolated. . . .

Precocious Sexuality

Sometimes a young child will have been taught by being sexually exploited that "favors" can be earned through sexual behavior. When Tom and Edna Smith went to visit Edna's sister, one of the sister's day-care children crawled up onto the couch where Tom was sitting. As the little girl reached over nonchalantly and unzipped Tom's pants, Tom was horrified, and he and Edna left the home immediately. Unfortunately, his surprise and disgust did not motivate him to pursue the incident further. Ten years later, when that little girl was 14 and pregnant, the crisis pregnancy center discovered that she had been sexually abused by her stepfather for several years as a child and had learned that sex was the way to get love and attention.[6]

 *Living Insights*   STUDY TWO

In another section of their book, Heitritter and Vought offer some key insights into how to help an abused child.

> More than any other variable, the reaction of the parents—or others who are important to the child—can have the greatest impact. "Experts agree that this is the single most important factor in preventing the abuse from becoming a life-destroying event."[7]

So what, specifically, should parents do? Here are eight helpful tips.

> 1. When a child discloses sexual abuse, try to remain calm. This will be difficult in light of the many feelings that will surface, but your feelings must be vented away from the child's presence. Do not overreact in front of the child.
> 2. Allow the child to describe, in his or her own words, what has physically happened. Do not ask questions that can be answered with yes or no, or suggest to the child what might have happened.

6. Heitritter and Vought, *Helping Victims of Sexual Abuse*, pp. 37–40. Used by permission.

7. Linda Tschirhart Sanford, *The Silent Children: A Parent's Guide to the Prevention of Child Sexual Abuse* (New York, N.Y.: McGraw-Hill, 1982), as quoted by Heitritter and Vought, *Helping Victims of Sexual Abuse*, p. 31.

Keep the number of persons interviewing the child to a minimum, both to protect the child from repeatedly having to expose the events of the abuse, and to protect the clarity of the details of the case, should it go to court.

3. Believe the child. Let the child describe the feelings resulting from the abuse and refrain from minimizing what has happened.

4. Assure the child that it was right to tell, and that he or she will be protected from the offender, if that is a threat. Protect the child's confidentiality against further trauma from peers or others at church, school, or the neighborhood.

5. Reassure the child repeatedly that the abuse was not his or her fault, that he or she is not to blame, and that he or she is not "bad" because the abuse happened. Reinforce that the offender is responsible for the abuse. Many times the child has a special relationship with the offender and has some positive feelings for him, so the child may defend the offender if you express intense or negative feelings about the offender.

6. Follow regular home routines. . . .

Under normal circumstances, children do not usually like changes in the routines of daily living. When major changes, such as moving away, follow sexual abuse incidents, it appears that the abuse is bigger than the family's ability to cope with it. This could increase the impact of the abuse on such a child.

7. Preserve normal physical affection. This is crucial in helping the child reestablish trust in adults and assurance of care and acceptance. If a child objects to affection, his or her boundaries should definitely be respected. At the same time, try to help him or her work through fears about affection and closeness.

8. Provide the child, and each family member, with support and counseling. When a child stops talking about the abuse after disclosure, it is often perceived by parents and others as a sign that the

issue has been resolved. Understandably, the family would like to forget about the abuse and get on with their lives, and telling a child to simply "forgive and forget" may temporarily soothe the family's pain. But if sufficient time isn't taken for the healing process, both the child and the family can be affected for life.[8]

8. Heitritter and Vought, *Helping Victims of Sexual Abuse*, pp. 33–34. Used by permission.

Chapter 6

CELEBRATE THE FEAST!

1 Corinthians 5:6–8

A Christian is the world's Bible," D. L. Moody once said, "and some of them need revising."[1] Ironically, the problem haunting many Christians today is not that we are ignored—it's that we're closely *observed*.

> You are writing a gospel,
>   A chapter each day,
> By deeds that you do,
>   By words that you say.
>
> Men read what you write,
>   Whether faithless or true;
> Say, what is the gospel
>   According to you?[2]

Much editing and revising is required for the world to see in each of us a uniquely inspired edition of personal purity. Collectively, the same is also true of Christ's body, the Church. Too often, we appear more like a flashy best-seller than a humble gospel, particularly when we titillate the public with the kind of pulp-novel behavior that existed in the first-century church of Corinth. A major revision was badly needed. Let's find out why from the pen of the apostle Paul.

> It is actually reported that there is immorality among you, and immorality of such a kind as does not exist even among the Gentiles, that someone has his father's wife. And you have become arrogant, and have not mourned instead, in order that the one who had done this deed might be removed from your midst. (1 Cor. 5:1–2)

A fitting title for the entire chapter introduced by this resolute

---

1. Dwight L. Moody, as quoted by Vance Havner in *The Best of Vance Havner* (1969; reprint, Grand Rapids, Mich.: Baker Book House, 1980), p. 28.

2. Paul Gilbert, "Your Own Version," in *The Best Loved Religious Poems*, comp. James Gilchrist Lawson (New York, N.Y.: Fleming H. Revell Co., 1933), p. 116.

indictment would be "How to Handle a Scandal." The church in Corinth was certainly caught up in one, but instead of handling the scandal, they condoned it! One of the believers was openly carrying on an incestuous affair with his stepmother, something even the pagan society of that day condemned. And worse than that, the Corinthian church was boasting about their broad-minded acceptance of his behavior.

"Shocked as he was at the sin," writes commentator William Barclay, "Paul was even more shocked by the attitude of the Corinthian Church to the sinner."[3] Their permissive indifference compelled the Apostle not only to pronounce judgment on this man (vv. 3–5) but also to strongly reprimand the church.[4]

> Your boasting is not good. Do you not know that a
> little leaven leavens the whole lump of dough? (v. 6)

Paul's appraisal of their attitude is even more jolting in the original Greek, which reverses the order of that first sentence to read "NOT GOOD is your boasting." The negative placed at the beginning of the sentence underscores its emphasis. The tone is that of a parent scolding a child: "You knew better than that. That's not good. You ought to be ashamed!" It's direct, forceful, and followed by a familiar truth they were taught as children in their homes but had failed to practice as adults in their church. The New International Version translates the passage this way: "Don't you know that a little yeast works through the whole batch of dough?"

"Here we have a picture expressed in Jewish terms," Barclay explains.

> With very few exceptions, leaven stands in Jewish
> literature for an evil influence. It was dough which
> had been kept over from a previous baking and
> which, in the keeping, had fermented. The Jews
> identified fermentation with putrefaction; and so
> leaven stood for a corrupting influence.[5]

---

3. William Barclay, *The Letters to the Corinthians*, rev. ed., The Daily Study Bible Series (Philadelphia, Pa.: Westminster Press, 1975), p. 44.

4. That Paul says nothing about disciplining the stepmother seems to indicate that she wasn't a believer.

5. Barclay, *The Letters to the Corinthians*, p. 45.

The leaven of the Corinthians' arrogant passivity toward the brother guilty of incest permeated the church, corrupting its witness. In fact, their lack of action actually made them a party to the sin, as commentators Robertson and Plummer note:

> To be indifferent to grave misbehaviour is to become partly responsible for it. A subtle atmosphere, in which evil readily springs up and is diffused, is the result.[6]

To restore their character as God's people would require correction, and Paul knew just what change they needed to make.

> Clean out the old leaven, that you may be a new lump, just as you are in fact unleavened. For Christ our Passover also has been sacrificed. (v. 7)

The Apostle's command is straightforward, but the reasoning behind it has some subtle connections with Jewish history:

> The Passover bread was unleavened. . . . More than that, on the day before the Passover Feast the law laid it down that the Jew must light a candle and search his house ceremonially for leaven, and that every last bit must be cast out. . . . Paul takes that picture. He says our sacrifice has been sacrificed, even Christ; it is his sacrifice which has delivered us from sin, as God delivered the Israelites from Egypt. Therefore, he goes on, the last remnant of evil must be cleared out of your lives. If you let an evil influence into the Church, it can corrupt the whole society, as the leaven permeates the whole lump of dough.[7]

In God's eyes, every individual who trusts in Christ is declared "unleavened," or righteous and clean (see Rom. 3:21–28; chap. 5; 8:1–2). The Corinthian believers themselves were unleavened, but their practice wasn't. Paul urges them to clean out the leaven so

6. Archibald Robertson and Alfred Plummer, A Critical and Exegetical Commentary on the First Epistle of St Paul to the Corinthians, 2d ed., International Critical Commentary series (1914; reprint, Edinburgh, Scotland: T. and T. Clark, 1971), p. 101.

7. Barclay, The Letters to the Corinthians, p. 45.

that their position and practice would once again present a harmonious message of holiness to the world.

Drawing his analogy and point to a close, the Apostle recommends,

> Let us therefore celebrate the feast, not with old leaven, nor with the leaven of malice and wickedness, but with the unleavened bread of sincerity and truth. (1 Cor. 5:8)

What was only an annual ritual for the Jew—cleansing the house of all leaven before Passover—is to be a daily reality for the Christian. Commentators Curtis Vaughan and Thomas Lea write:

> The Corinthians are to remove the leaven of malice and evil, the standards of the old life. They are to show the sincerity that comes from pure motives and the godly action that results from practicing the truth. The sin from which they had been rescued must be a thing of the past, and holiness must become the abiding quality of the present and future.[8]

Frederic Godet once said, "The Christian's [Passover] feast does not last a week, but all his life."[9] As you think about celebrating that feast by cleaning the leaven out of your own life, remember these two practical applications.

First, *it is harder to get our lives clean than to keep them clean.* A house that's been dirty for months takes a lot more work to clean than one that was just dusted and vacuumed yesterday. In the same way, a life long permeated with the leaven of sin is much more difficult to cleanse than a life kept clean by confession on a daily basis. It's harder to catch up than it is to keep up.

Second, *periodically, a complete inner cleansing is necessary.* Did you know that the Passover ritual of searching for leaven is looked upon as the origin of our spring-cleaning? If you've ever done one, you'll remember how you always make surprising discoveries as you clean every nook and cranny of the house. Like our homes, our lives often become cluttered with things—thoughts, habits,

---

8. Curtis Vaughan and Thomas D. Lea, *1 Corinthians*, Bible Study Commentary Series (Grand Rapids, Mich.: Zondervan Publishing House, Lamplighter Books, 1983), p. 59.

9. Frederic Louis Godet, *Commentary on First Corinthians* (Grand Rapids, Mich.: Kregel Publications, 1977), p. 266.

motives—that rarely catch our attention unless we conduct a "spring-cleaning" from time to time. Perhaps once a year, set aside an extended period of time to allow yourself to look deeply into the corners and beneath the familiar practices to see if any leaven has collected that needs to be thrown out.

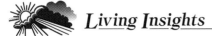 ## *Living Insights*

Spring-cleaning. As a child, that word caused great weeping and gnashing of teeth in my home. To my brother, my two sisters, and me, spring-cleaning was the final Apocalypse, Judgment Day, the end of life as we knew it. Condemned to hard labor, we beseeched our mother with mournful basset-hound eyes for a postponement of this grievous injustice. Scrubbing tile, cleaning ovens, reorganizing shelves, wiping down baseboards—this was cruel and unusual punishment! No kind, loving, her-children-rise-up-and-call-her-blessed mother would force her son or daughter to do such things. "Would you, Mom?"

That was our mistake. What we didn't realize was that we weren't talking to *our* mother anymore. She had gone wherever real mothers go during spring-cleaning (Tahiti, I think), and in her place stood someone who looked like our mother but was really a taskmaster from ancient Egypt. And not Moses himself nor all the plagues of heaven were going to free us from our bitter bondage until every dust ball, every cobweb, every grease smudge had been completely cleansed from Egypt.

Thank goodness we all grew up. That was our only deliverance —adulthood. But you know, since becoming a Christian, I've discovered the need for another kind of spring-cleaning, one that's actually a wonderful experience no believer ever outgrows. Keeping our spiritual house clean requires not only a daily effort but also an occasional respite of uninterrupted fellowship with the Lord. By slowing down through prayer, scriptural meditation, worship, and reflection, we can restore our perspective and see the leaven we normally miss because we're too distracted by life's busyness.

As your shepherd, Jesus wants you to lie down in green pastures, beside still waters, so He can restore your soul. Would you take a moment right now to plan a spiritual retreat for you and the Lord to get away and do just that?

When?_____ Where?_____

If you've never done this before, let me suggest that you seek a godly mentor who could provide you with some spiritual direction for your time away.[10]

Now, about that other spring-cleaning you've been putting off. Relax, you're an adult! You don't have to do that anymore—your kids can! (See you in Tahiti.)

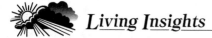 *Living Insights*

I looked under the couch the other day while on another of those desperate searches for the car keys. Naturally, they weren't there, but a really disgusting green-and-black lump was. I stared hard, hoping this "thing" would come into focus so I could put a name to it. But nothing in my vocabulary fit this fuzzy anomaly. That's when I started feeling a little alarmed. What *is* that? Maybe if I touch it . . . no, don't touch. Think. Something the dog buried? A new life form?

Whatever it was, I realized I couldn't just leave it now that I had seen it. Once you uncover something smutchy like that, you can't just walk away and pretend you never saw it. You have to deal with it, right? Just like those small, hidden sins in our lives. When the Spirit of God does a little housecleaning and exposes something swept under the rug, we've got to deal with it, right?

Maybe. Many Christians do, but then many of us take the attitude that a little leaven is no big deal so long as we keep it where others can't see it. But is it the size or hiddenness of our sin that determines whether we should clear it out, or is it the awesome holiness of our Lord?

Are you putting off cleaning up an attitude or a habit simply because no one else knows about it? "Clean out the old leaven, that you may be a new lump, just as you are in fact unleavened," Paul urges (1 Cor. 5:7a). Dedicate yourself to that right now by asking God to sensitize you to those hidden sins, using the words from Psalm 139:23–24 as an opening prayer.

---

10. "Spiritual direction" for individuals and groups is a centuries-old tradition within the Church. Today's evangelicals are rediscovering this practice through ministries such as Renovaré, 8 Inverness Drive East, Suite 102, Englewood, Colorado 80112-5624, (303) 792-0146.

Becoming a "new lump," as Paul encourages us to do, may not sound all that appealing; but if you had only seen the lump that had been hidden under my couch, you would be very motivated.

What was that ominous green-and-black thing? Why, my son's half-eaten apple, of course. The one I had asked him to throw away three weeks ago.

Chapter 7

CURING THE PLAGUE OF DEATH

Ecclesiastes 3; Romans 5

The Great Plague that infected London in the seventeenth century began innocuously enough with a few isolated cases in May 1664. One year later in that same month, 590 cases were reported, but ignored. By June the number swelled to 6,137. Panic ensued as the figure rose to 17,000 in July. Like stampeding cattle, two-thirds of London's population fled their homes as the deaths totaled 31,000 in August, 1665. But that was only the beginning. By the time the Plague was brought under control, more than 70,000 Londoners had been buried or burned.

What caused this catastrophe? The infinitesimal bites of fleas carried by diseased rats. Back then, however, people thought bad-smelling air was the problem, so they carried sweet-scented posy petals in their pockets to ward off the disease. Hospitals even walked patients around rose gardens hoping to cleanse their lungs with the flowers' fragrance. This cured no one, of course, and it's said that one man sang these words as he piled the victims onto his pushcart:

> Ring around the roses,
> A pocket full of posies;
> Ashes, ashes, we all fall down.[1]

Ironically, this parody of calamity is now sung all over the world as an innocent nursery rhyme. Yet for those who know the horror of its history, the last line is a sobering reminder of the greatest plague of all—death.

Even those fortunate enough to escape the Plague in that day still eventually died. "Death is a debt we all must pay," wrote the Greek poet Euripides.[2] "Ashes, ashes, we all fall down" is also a constant refrain throughout the Scriptures.

---

1. As told by Charles R. Swindoll in *Come Before Winter . . . and Share My Hope* (Portland, Oreg.: Multnomah Press, 1985), p. 34.

2. Euripides, as quoted in *The Home Book of Quotations*, 10th ed., comp. Burton Stevenson (New York, N.Y.: Dodd, Mead and Co., 1967), p. 377.

"By the sweat of your face
You shall eat bread,
Till you return to the ground,
Because from it you were taken;
For you are dust,
And to dust you shall return." (Gen. 3:19)

What man can live and not see death?
(Ps. 89:48a)

It is appointed for men to die once and after this
comes judgment. (Heb. 9:27; see also James 4:14)

Examination: Cures in Contrast

Despite death's obvious and inevitable reality, it is still difficult
for most of us to accept our own mortality. Over the centuries,
philosophies have been prescribed to cope with death and its impact
on the meaning of life. Six in particular are hinted at in Ecclesiastes 3.

Human Philosophy

1. *Fatalism* (vv. 1–9): This bleak belief is often called the "doctrine of despair." It teaches that events are fixed in advance for all
time and follow a blind, irrational process that leaves humankind
without meaning, responsibility, or significance.

2. *Skepticism* (vv. 10–11): "Man will not find out the work
which God has done" is the central theme behind this way of
thinking. Nothing can be known for certain, the skeptic says. Everything supposedly certain is suspect; doubt is the way of life. One
particular strain of this thinking is agnosticism, which states that
God is unknowable and inexpressible.

3. *Hedonism* (vv. 12–13): The followers of this lifestyle devote
themselves to the pursuit of personal pleasure. There is no life after
death, no punishment for sins, so they live for today and don't worry
about the future. "Eat, drink, and be merry, for tomorrow we may
die" is their guiding principle (see 1 Cor. 15:32).

4. *Deism* (vv. 14–17): Adherents of this belief say God created
the world to run according to natural laws without His supernatural
interference. This concept denies the possibility of miracles, including the greatest one of all—God becoming flesh in Christ to offer
Himself up as the sacrifice for our sins.

5. *Evolutionism* (vv. 18–19): We are but animals evolved from

62

prehistoric primordial slime. Chance and change are the rulers of our fate. This life is all there is; death is final.

6. *Universalism* (vv. 20–22): "All go to the same place." Solomon says that place is the dust of the earth. Universalists, on the other hand, believe that everyone will be resurrected to live happily ever after in heaven with God. No need to worry about sin, judgment, or hell. All men and women are promised the same wonderful paradise sometime in the future.

Proverbs 14:12 says, "There is a way which seems right to a man, But its end is the way of death." The Hebrew term for *right* means "smooth, pleasing, agreeable." Each of the philosophies listed have seemed plausible and palatable to people throughout the ages. But none of them are God's way, and they are no more effective in curing the plague of death than putting posies in our pockets or circling rose beds.

Divine Remedy

In contrast to the various humanistic elixirs sold over the world's counter, God offers a sure remedy for death in His Word. Let's turn to Romans 5 and listen carefully as He examines our condition and prescribes the cure.

The truth. Beginning in verse 12, we're given a brief case history of death.

> Therefore, just as through one man sin entered
> into the world, and death through sin, and so death
> spread to all men, because all sinned.

The plague originated through the disobedience of one man (Adam), the immediate result was that "sin entered into the world," and the ultimate end was that "death spread to all."

The formula. We could take the truths of this verse and translate them into this simple formula:

$$\text{Humanity} + \text{Iniquity} = \text{Depravity}$$

We are all "under sin" (Gal. 3:22), and that puts us in the worst possible position before a holy God. This same truth is underscored by three other terms used to describe the unsaved in this chapter— "helpless" (Rom. 5:6), "sinners" (v. 8), and "enemies" (v. 10).

The hope. Helpless sinners. Enemies of God. The diagnosis of our condition is depressing. However, "God, being rich in mercy, because of His great love with which He loved us," offered a cure to save us from our hopeless destiny with death (Eph. 2:4). Read the prescription recommended in verses 17–21 of Romans 5:

> For if by the transgression of the one, death reigned through the one, much more those who receive the abundance of grace and of the gift of righteousness will reign in life through the One, Jesus Christ. So then as through one transgression there resulted condemnation to all men, even so through one act of righteousness there resulted justification of life to all men. For as through the one man's disobedience the many were made sinners, even so through the obedience of the One the many will be made righteous. And the Law came in that the transgression might increase; but where sin increased, grace abounded all the more, that, as sin reigned in death, even so grace might reign through righteousness to eternal life through Jesus Christ our Lord.

The plague of death has only one cure—Jesus Christ. Notice the five specific ways in which He brings healing.

ROMANS 5 SUMMARIZED

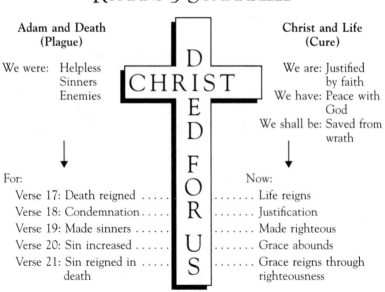

Adam and Death
(Plague)

We were: Helpless
Sinners
Enemies

For:
Verse 17: Death reigned .....
Verse 18: Condemnation.....
Verse 19: Made sinners ......
Verse 20: Sin increased ......
Verse 21: Sin reigned in .....
death

Christ and Life
(Cure)

We are: Justified
by faith
We have: Peace with
God
We shall be: Saved from
wrath

Now:
.... Life reigns
.... Justification
.... Made righteous
.... Grace abounds
.... Grace reigns through
righteousness

What assurance do we have that Christ's treatment of the plague of death really works? An empty tomb. As Josh McDowell writes:

> All but four of the major world religions are based on mere philosophical propositions. Of the four that are based on personalities rather than a philosophical system, only Christianity claims an empty tomb for its founder.[3]

Muhammad's grave is occupied. So is Buddha's. Even Abraham, the father of Judaism, still rests in the dust. But not Christ.

> [He] has been raised from the dead, the first fruits of those who are asleep. For since by a man came death, by a man also came the resurrection of the dead. (1 Cor. 15:20–21)

Rose beds and posy pedals are no cure for death. Only Jesus, the risen Savior, has overcome the plague to add a new line of hope to the rhyme:

> Ring around the roses,
> A pocket full of posies;
> Ashes, ashes, we all fall down.
> In Christ, however, all shall be made alive!
> (see 1 Cor. 15:22)

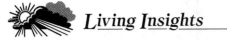 *Living Insights*   STUDY ONE

Do you ever struggle to make sense out of life? Many of us, even though we're Christians, sometimes wonder if God really is personally involved with the human race, or if we really can know anything for sure, or if maybe we are here by chance and don't really have any meaning after all. You know what? When we feel this way, which is usually when we're pretty far down in the dumps, we're unwittingly buying into the humanistic philosophies of deism, skepticism, or evolutionism.

As you look back to some recent discouraging times, can you

---

3. Josh McDowell, comp., *Evidence That Demands a Verdict*, rev. ed. (San Bernardino, Calif.: Here's Life Publishers, 1979), p. 180.

detect any of these humanistic philosophies creeping in to chill your heart? Name them, and describe what they usually say to you.

_____

_____

_____

_____

_____

Because humanistic philosophies can offer no real hope, we are left feeling more discouraged and dead. But Christ's remedy is different, isn't it? He not only provides life after death but revives our hearts now and makes us alive inside.

Using our passage from Romans 5, as well as Ephesians 2:1–10, write a response to each of the humanistic philosophies that plague you. In doing this, you will guard your heart from the world's despair and the Tempter's snare (compare Matt. 4:1–11).

_____

_____

_____

_____

_____

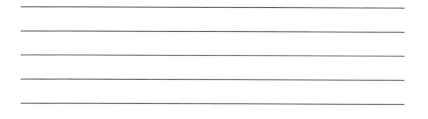 **Living Insights** STUDY TWO

"No, not me, it cannot be true." In her book *On Death and Dying*, Elisabeth Kübler-Ross says most of the patients she interviewed responded like that when first told they were terminally ill.[4] Denial is a coping mechanism, our first line of defense against such traumatic news. Dr. Kübler-Ross recalls the story of one particular middle-aged woman she met at the hospital.

Repeated visits made it obvious that she feared any

---

4. Elisabeth Kübler-Ross, *On Death and Dying* (New York, N.Y.: Macmillan Publishing Co., 1969), p. 38.

communications from staff members, who might possibly break down her denial, i.e., talk about her advanced cancer. As she grew weaker, her makeup became more grotesque. Originally rather discretely applied red lipstick and rouge, the makeup became brighter and redder until she resembled a clown. Her clothing became equally brighter and more colorful as her end approached. During the last few days she avoided looking in a mirror, but continued to apply the masquerade in an attempt to cover up her increasing depression and her rapidly deteriorating looks.[5]

In sharing the gospel with others, it's likely we will hear, "No, not me, it cannot be true," many times in many ways. The whole world is basically in denial of Christ. Can you see any parallels between this woman's struggle to deny death and perhaps the way a non-Christian friend is acting out his or her denial of sin and the need for a Savior?

_____

_____

_____

What insights do your observations give you as to how to pray for and approach this person?

_____

_____

_____

_____

5. Kübler-Ross, On Death and Dying, pp. 40–41.

Chapter 8

CLAIMING THE
PROMISE OF LIFE
Acts 2:22–38

Jesus was not God. He was only a man born at a crucial moment in Jewish history who manipulated people and events to make it appear as if he were the Messiah. His clever schemes went awry, though, and he became a victim of the very plot he had endeavored to promote.

So says Dr. Hugh J. Schonfield in his book *The Passover Plot.* It was published in the mid-sixties and caused quite a hullabaloo in the Christian community and the world. Admittedly, it had a certain appeal. The thesis was well-stated, and more importantly, it provided non-Christians an authoritative voice to rally around in support of their unbelief.

One glaring chink does exist, however, in Dr. Schonfield's refutation. Chuck Swindoll observed it firsthand as he listened to the author answer questions after a lecture at Brandeis University. A Jewish student stood and asked the simple six-word question: "How do you explain the Resurrection?" A period of silence ensued in which Dr. Schonfield cleared his throat, squirmed a little, and then passed off the question as unimportant. But the student wasn't to be denied. A little later he stood for a second time, saying, "Dr. Schonfield, you're avoiding the question. How do you explain the Resurrection?" "That really isn't a significant question," he replied and moved on to another question. Determined, the student stood for a third time. "Will you please be seated?" Dr. Schonfield asked. "No, sir," the student answered. "How do you explain the Resurrection?" And the authority who supposedly exposed Jesus as a fraud simply ignored the question.

But the Resurrection cannot be ignored. As Michael Green explained in *Man Alive!,*

> Christianity does not hold the resurrection to be one among many tenets of belief. Without faith in the resurrection *there would be no Christianity at all.* The Christian church would never have begun; the Jesus-movement would have fizzled out like a damp squib

with his execution. Christianity stands or falls with the truth of the resurrection. Once disprove it, and you have disposed of Christianity.[1]

One scholar noted that even caustic critics, such as D. F. Strauss, acknowledge that the Resurrection "touches all Christianity to the quick," and is "decisive for the whole view of Christianity."[2] John Mackintosh Shaw says, "If this goes, all that is vital and essential in Christianity goes; if this remains, all else remains. And so through the centuries, from Celsus onwards, the Resurrection has been the storm centre of the attack upon the Christian faith."[3]

How, then, could Dr. Schonfield consider that student's question too inconsequential to answer? How could he have missed the Mount Everest of the apostles' teaching concerning Christ? Incredible, isn't it? It will seem all the more so after we examine the apostle Peter's unforgettable presentation of the gospel in Acts 2.

Background

It was morning, sometime just before nine o'clock. Peter and the rest of the disciples were in Jerusalem patiently waiting, praying, just as Jesus had told them to do, when . . .

> suddenly there came from heaven a noise like a violent, rushing wind, and it filled the whole house where they were sitting. And there appeared to them tongues as of fire distributing themselves, and they rested on each one of them. And they were all filled with the Holy Spirit and began to speak with other tongues, as the Spirit was giving them utterance. (vv. 2–4)

The sound of the disciples' voices immediately attracted a multitude of "bewildered" and "amazed" listeners (vv. 6, 7). "How is it that we each hear them in our own language?" the people wondered (v. 8). "What does this mean?" (v. 12). "It means these men are drunk and babbling nothing but nonsense," some people mocked (see v. 13).

---

1. Michael Green, *Man Alive!* (1967; reprint, Chicago, Ill.: Inter-Varsity Press, 1968), p. 55.

2. As quoted by John Mackintosh Shaw in "Resurrection of Christ," in *Dictionary of the Apostolic Church*, ed. James Hastings (New York, N.Y.: Charles Scribner's Sons, 1918), vol. 2, p. 330.

3. Shaw, "Resurrection," *Dictionary of the Apostolic Church*, vol. 2, p. 330.

That was Peter's cue. Like the Jewish student who stood up against Dr. Schonfield, Peter took his stand with the eleven and confidently delivered a convicting message we might appropriately title "How Do You Explain the Resurrection?"

Five Salient Points

The Apostle's sermon falls basically into two parts. First, in verses 14–21, he answers the accusation that they were drunk by using a quotation from the Old Testament. Then, in verses 22–36, Peter recounts Christ's story, leading up to the climax of His Resurrection. Beginning with verse 22, let's follow the progressive key points of that powerful message.

1. Christ's Humiliation

> "Men of Israel, listen to these words: Jesus the Nazarene, a man attested to you by God . . ." (v. 22a)

Don't overlook the impact of these first few words. It had been less than two months since Christ was crucified. These were Jesus' contemporaries Peter was addressing. Many of them had probably heard Him teach, seen Him heal, or watched Him die. The mere mention of His name still excited and agitated people. Knowing this, Peter reminded them that God had "attested" to this man, meaning He had exhibited Him or put Him on display. In Philippians 2, the apostle Paul describes the humbling process Jesus the Lord God went through to become Jesus the Nazarene, the man who exhibited God among the people.

> Have this attitude in yourselves which was also in Christ Jesus, who, although He existed in the form of God, did not regard equality with God a thing to be grasped, but emptied Himself, taking the form of a bondservant, and being made in the likeness of men. (Phil. 2:5–7)

2. Christ's Incarnation

Next, Peter stirred their memories to show them the link between Jesus and God.

> ". . . a man attested to you by God with miracles and wonders and signs which God performed through Him in your midst, just as you yourselves

know." (Acts 2:22b)

God proved that Jesus was no mere man, the Apostle reminded them. Don't you remember the five thousand He fed, and the widow's son in Nain He raised from the dead, and the countless sick and disabled bodies He healed? Only someone divinely empowered could do such miracles. The stamp of deity rested upon Christ. You saw His works; you know it's true.

3. Christ's Crucifixion

> "This Man, delivered up by the predetermined plan and foreknowledge of God, you nailed to a cross by the hands of godless men and put Him to death." (v. 23)

Like the nails driven into Christ's hands and feet, Peter drove the truth of the Crucifixion into the hearts of his listeners. Jesus' death was no accident. No one forced that on Him, nor was it a last desperate option after all others had run out. God's Son allowed Himself to be killed because that had been the Father's plan from the beginning (see also 3:18; 4:27–28; 13:29).

Equally true, however, was the fact that the Crucifixion was a heinous crime, and the guilt for it lay not in the abstract realm of God's sovereignty or in the fulfillment of Scripture. Rather, the bold fisherman placed it squarely on the shoulders of the very people hearing his voice: "*You* nailed Him to the cross. *You're* responsible for His death."

4. Christ's Resurrection

The pangs of remorse went deep into the consciences of many who were listening. Yet Peter did not leave them there, crucified by their own guilt. He immediately took them to the cornerstone of Christianity's faith and hope—the empty tomb.

> "And God raised Him up again, putting an end to the agony of death, since it was impossible for Him to be held in its power. For David says of Him,
> 'I was always beholding the Lord in my
> presence;
> For He is at my right hand, that I may not
> be shaken.
> Therefore my heart was glad and my tongue
> exulted;

71

Moreover my flesh also will abide in hope;
Because Thou wilt not abandon my soul to
    Hades,
Nor allow Thy Holy One to undergo decay.
Thou hast made known to me the ways of
    life;
Thou wilt make me full of gladness with Thy
    presence.'
Brethren, I may confidently say to you regarding the
patriarch David that he both died and was buried,
and his tomb is with us to this day. And so, because
he was a prophet, and knew that God had sworn to
him with an oath to seat one of his descendants
upon his throne, he looked ahead and spoke of the
resurrection of the Christ, that He was neither abandoned to Hades, nor did His flesh suffer decay. This
Jesus God raised up again, to which we are all witnesses." (2:24–32)

Sandwiched between the two declarations "God raised Him up"
(v. 24) and "God raised up" (v. 32) is a quotation from Psalm 16.
Some have said David is speaking of himself, but verses 29–32 of
Acts 2 make it clear that David is prophesying about the Messiah.
The apostle Paul gave this same interpretation in a message delivered at the synagogue in Pisidian Antioch (see Acts 13:13–41).
And who was that Messiah? Anyone could claim to be Him. The
final proof of Jesus' identity as the Anointed One was the Resurrection. And to confirm that fact, Peter added that they were witnesses to His having been raised (2:32).

5. Christ's Exaltation

Drawing his message to a close, Peter tied together all that the
people had seen and heard that morning to a final truth concerning
Christ.

"Therefore having been exalted to the right hand of
God, and having received from the Father the promise of the Holy Spirit, He has poured forth this which
you both see and hear. For it was not David who
ascended into heaven, but he himself says:
    'The Lord said to my lord,
      "Sit at My right hand,

Until I make Thine enemies a footstool for
Thy feet."'
Therefore let all the house of Israel know for certain
that God has made Him both Lord and Christ—
this Jesus whom you crucified." (vv. 33–36)

The people could hear the certainty of what Peter said in his
voice, in his confidence, and, most importantly, in their own hearts.
No one doubted the glorious truth of the Messiah's exaltation. And
it absolutely terrified them.

Response

Now when they heard this, they were pierced to
the heart, and said to Peter and the rest of the apostles, "Brethren, what shall we do?" (v. 37)

Unfortunately, many non-Christians who ask that same question today are told that they must earn God's favor by doing good
works—practice self-denial, do penance, follow a particular list of
dos and don'ts. But no matter whose standards we may follow or
how much good we may achieve, we can never reach perfection or
atone for even one of our sins. Only Jesus' blood shed on the cross
for you and me makes forgiveness possible (see Heb. 9:11–14, 22).
Salvation cannot be won by works, Paul says in Ephesians 2:8–9,
only received as a free gift through faith in Christ. He is the resurrection and the life, those who believe in Him shall live even if
they die (John 11:25). This is the gospel, the true message of Christ's
humiliation, incarnation, crucifixion, resurrection, and exaltation.
Peter knew this, and he quenched the thirsty souls beseeching him
with the living water of Jesus.

And Peter said to them, "Repent, and let each of
you be baptized in the name of Jesus Christ for the
forgiveness of your sins; and you shall receive the
gift of the Holy Spirit." (Acts 2:38)

The difference between fact and fiction, between Peter's message and the message of *The Passover Plot,* is an empty tomb. Living
Lord or deluded pretender—how do you explain the Resurrection?

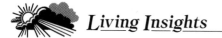

Adolf Harnack, who rejects the Church's belief in
the resurrection, admits: "The firm confidence of the
disciples in Jesus was rooted in the belief that He
did not abide in death, but was raised by God. That
Christ was risen . . . became the main article of
their preaching about Him."[4]

Just how central was the Resurrection in the apostles' preaching
and defense of the gospel? Let's find out for ourselves by revisiting some
key moments in the expansion of the early Church, recorded in Acts.
Read each of the following passages and note the important specifics.

Acts 3 _____

_____

Acts 4:1–12 _____

_____

Acts 5:12–32 _____

_____

Acts 10:1–43 _____

_____

Acts 13:13–41 _____

_____

Acts 17:16–34 _____

_____

Acts 25:13–26:29 _____

_____

---

4. E. Hermitage Day, *On the Evidence for the Resurrection* (London, England: Society for
Promoting Christian Knowledge, 1906); as quoted by Josh McDowell, comp., *Evidence That
Demands a Verdict*, rev. ed. (San Bernardino, Calif.: Here's Life Publishers, 1979), p. 181.

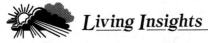 *Living Insights*

God arranged a perfect plan to deal with sin and death:

His Son—
    His death—
        His resurrection—
that we might know, personally, His life.

But how? What shall we do to experience His life personally? First and foremost, as William Barclay noted in his commentary, Peter said to repent (Acts 2:38). What did the Apostle mean by that? Barclay explains:

> The word originally meant an *afterthought*. Often a second thought shows that the first thought was wrong; and so the word came to mean *a change of mind*. But, if a man is an honest man, a change of mind demands *a change of action*. Repentance must involve both change of mind and change of action. A man may change his mind and come to see that his actions were wrong but be so much in love with his old ways that he will not change them. A man may change his ways but his mind remains the same, changing only because of fear or prudence. True repentance involves a change of mind *and* a change of action.[5]

If all we want is a moral philosophy, we need only change our thinking. If we desire a respectable religion, simple outward conformity will do. But, if we want to know Christ intimately, we must change our minds *and* actions. Which version of repentance are you practicing?

5. William Barclay, *The Acts of the Apostles*, rev. ed., The Daily Study Bible Series (Philadelphia, Pa.: Westminster Press, 1976), pp. 28–29.

Chapter 9

LIFE'S TURNING POINTS

Acts 9:1–22

David kills Goliath.
  Abraham offers his son Isaac as a sacrifice.
    Jacob wrestles with an angel.
      Jonah is swallowed by a great fish.
        Joseph's brothers sell him into slavery.
Pivotal moments. Proverbial forks in the road. *Turning points.*
Much of life meanders peacefully in the slow currents of eating,
sleeping, mowing the grass, and paying bills—nothing very exciting
or unusual. But there are those rare moments when something so
significant, so traumatic, so extraordinary happens that we are never
the same afterward.

Although giants, angels, and scaly leviathans are not a typical
part of most people's turning points, at least four traits are common
in this kind of an experience.

General Observations about Turning Points

Four factors especially stand out in all turning points:

- First, they occur during the normal course of events.

- Second, they are usually sudden and unexpected, leaving us
  shocked and confused.

- Third, they impact others whose lives are interwoven with ours.

- And fourth, they prompt changes in us that surprise others.

Case in point—the crossroads confrontation Saul of Tarsus experienced on a first-century thoroughfare to Damascus.

Saul's Turning Point on the Damascus Road

Personal epiphanies like the one that transformed Saul's life are
rare. Rarer still do we get to revisit them as actual eyewitnesses. In
Acts 9, however, we're given just that chance. Beginning with verse 1,
let's acquaint ourselves with this Pharisee and then join him on a
journey to Damascus. He has important orders to carry out and is

in a hurry to reach his destination; and he'll get there—but with a completely different destiny.

His Lifestyle and Objective

> Now Saul, still breathing threats and murder against the disciples of the Lord . . . (v. 1a)

For those of you who don't know much about Saul, he was a highly educated, high-profile Pharisee, one of the religious elite of his day. He had a passion for his ancestors' faith and advanced in Judaism beyond many of his contemporaries (see Gal. 1:13–14). And, as you can see from what Luke wrote, he absolutely *hated* Christians. From the time of Stephen's stoning (Acts 7), Saul "began ravaging the church, entering house after house; and dragging off men and women, he would put them in prison" (8:3).

In *The Man Who Shook the World*, John Pollock aptly writes of Saul:

> He charged like an animal tearing its prey. This was not the sad efficiency of an officer obeying distasteful orders; the heart was engaged. . . . Every suspect, man or woman, had to stand before the elders while [Saul], as the High Priest's representative, put to them the demand that they should curse Jesus. . . .
>
> He threw them into dungeons. One or two may have been stoned. . . . The majority were punished by public flogging, the "forty stripes save one" which was no sight for the squeamish. . . .
>
> He remained unmoved as men—and women—staggered away with backs a mass of weals and blood. He was equally unmoved by the refusal of grown men to be humiliated by a beating in front of neighbors.[1]

Commentator A. T. Robertson adds, "Threatening and slaughter had come to be the very breath that Saul breathed, like a warhorse who sniffed the smell of battle."[2] For a time, that "smell of battle" lay exclusively over the church in Jerusalem. But eventually,

---

1. John Pollock, *The Man Who Shook the World* (Wheaton, Ill.: Scripture Press Publications, Victor Books, 1972), pp. 13–15.

2. Archibald Thomas Robertson, *Word Pictures in the New Testament* (Grand Rapids, Mich.: Baker Book House, 1930), vol. 3, p. 113.

Saul's lust for blood drew him to pursue those who had fled perse-cution into the neighboring regions of Judea and Samaria. So, he went to the high priest

> and asked for letters from him to the synagogues at Damascus, so that if he found any belonging to the Way, both men and women, he might bring them bound to Jerusalem. (9:2)

This was a man on a mission. Damascus was a hundred and forty miles away! Undaunted, Saul packed his extradition orders and set off with an accompanying police force to haul back all the fugitive believers he could find.

Sudden Intervention and Saul's Reaction

Remember the four observations we made about turning points? The first was that they occur during the normal course of events.

> And it came about that as he journeyed, he was approaching Damascus. (v. 3a)

Now put yourself on that dusty road with Saul and watch the second observation unfold.

> Suddenly a light from heaven flashed around him; and he fell to the ground, and heard a voice saying to him, "Saul, Saul, why are you persecuting Me?" And he said, "Who art Thou, Lord?" And He said, "I am Jesus whom you are persecuting." (vv. 3b–5)

Listen again as Pollock recaptures this dramatic moment.

> [Saul] could not believe what he heard and saw. All his convictions, intellect and training, his reputa-tion, his self-respect, demanded that Jesus should not be alive again. He played for time and replied, "Who are you, Lord?" He used a mode of address which might mean no more than "Your honor."
> "I am Jesus, whom you are persecuting. . . ."
> Then he knew. In a second that seemed an eter-nity [Saul] saw the wounds in Jesus' hands and feet, saw the face and knew that he had seen the Lord, that he was alive, as Stephen and the others had said. . . .

[Saul] had never admitted to himself that he had felt pricks of a goad as he raged against Stephen and his disciples. But now, instantaneously, he was shatteringly aware that he had been fighting Jesus. And fighting himself, his conscience, his powerlessness, the darkness and chaos in his soul. God hovered over this chaos and brought him to the moment of new creation. It wanted only his "Yes."

[Saul] broke.

He was trembling and in no state to weigh the pros and cons of changing sides. He only knew that he had heard a voice and had seen the Lord, and that nothing mattered but to find and obey his will.[3]

This was Saul's crossroad of conversion, the turning point that quite literally separated darkness from light in his life. Once a proud Pharisee, now a helpless newborn believer, he then took his first baby steps toward a new destiny.

"Rise, and enter the city, and it shall be told you what you must do." And the men who traveled with him stood speechless, hearing the voice, but seeing no one. And Saul got up from the ground, and though his eyes were open, he could see nothing; and leading him by the hand, they brought him into Damascus. And he was three days without sight, and neither ate nor drank. (vv. 6–9)

Ananias' Involvement and God's Revelation

Still reeling from his revelation, Saul patiently waits while the Lord orchestrates the third characteristic of a turning point: where someone else's life is impacted.

Now there was a certain disciple at Damascus, named Ananias; and the Lord said to him in a vision, "Ananias." And he said, "Behold, here am I, Lord." And the Lord said to him, "Arise and go to the street called Straight, and inquire at the house of Judas for a man from Tarsus named Saul, for behold, he is praying, and he has seen in a vision a man named

---

3. Pollock, *The Man Who Shook the World*, p. 18.

Ananias come in and lay his hands on him, so that he might regain his sight." (vv. 10–12)

Ananias was impacted, all right—with fear!

But Ananias answered, "Lord, I have heard from many about this man, how much harm he did to Thy saints at Jerusalem; and here he has authority from the chief priests to bind all who call upon Thy name." (vv. 13–14)

Ananias is afraid, and rightly so. Christians don't lay hands on Saul of Tarsus; he lays his on them and throws them into prison or has them beaten, or both.

But the Lord said to him, "Go, for he is a chosen instrument of Mine, to bear My name before the Gentiles and kings and the sons of Israel; for I will show him how much he must suffer for My name's sake." (vv. 15–16)

Formerly a blasphemer, persecutor, and violent aggressor, now Saul is Christ's "chosen instrument." What an incredible example of God's inestimable grace. Would Ananias have the faith to demonstrate that grace by seeking out his former enemy? The answer is revealed in three simple words, "And Ananias departed" (v. 17a). Let's follow this unsung hero as he fulfills God's mission of mercy.

Saul's Changes and Others' Surprise

Ananias departed and entered the house, and after laying his hands on him said, "Brother Saul, the Lord Jesus, who appeared to you on the road by which you were coming, has sent me so that you may regain your sight, and be filled with the Holy Spirit." (v. 17)

That must have been an incredible moment, not only for Ananias, whose knees were probably knocking, but also for Saul. What was the first word he heard? *Brother*—a warm, accepting term of endearment from someone he'd set out to persecute. This triggers the fourth characteristic in Saul's turning point, changes that surprise others. Have a look.

1. He immediately regained his eyesight (v. 18a).

2. Shortly thereafter he was baptized (v. 18b).

3. Next, he spent time fellowshiping with the disciples in Damascus (v. 19b).

4. After that, he began proclaiming in the synagogues that Jesus was the Son of God (v. 20).

5. He kept increasing in strength and persuasive wisdom, proving that Jesus is the Christ (v. 22).

Amazing, isn't it? What a transformation. This isn't Saul, the hate-filled Pharisee who charged like a wild animal to tear its prey. This is a new creature, a new life, a new brother. This is the apostle Paul.

When Your Turning Point Occurs

Everyone's life has turning points. Not all of them are as spiritually dramatic as Paul's, but they are life-changing just the same. God steps into our lives and touches an area that is lacking. Something sudden and unexpected happens *to us*, but it is not nearly so significant as what happens *in us*.

More than just exposing our need, however, God wants to supply the balm of His help to heal and make us whole. He transformed Saul from a pit bull persecutor into the humble apostle Paul, a chosen instrument set apart to bear His name before Jews, Gentiles, and kings. Just imagine, then, what He could do for you!

"But my life is just so boring and routine," you say? Hmmm. What was that first observation about turning points?

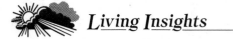 *Living Insights* STUDY ONE

Has there been a turning point in your life? Though most of us may have experienced one, few people ever take the time to really examine the details of what happened by writing them down. We'd like to give you that opportunity now. Using as your guide the four characteristics of a turning point from our lesson, re-create the significant details surrounding your own personal story.

My Turning Point

The Normal Course of Events

_____

_____

_____

_____

_____

_____

The Sudden and Unexpected That Left Me Shocked and Confused

_____

_____

_____

_____

_____

_____

The Impact on Others Whose Lives Were Interwoven with Mine

_____

_____

_____

_____

_____

The Changes Prompted in Me That Surprised Others

_____

_____

_____

_____

_____

Though your crossroads experience may have happened years

ago, reliving it may still prompt you to praise God or to write a thank-you note to someone who, like Ananias, played a key role in your life at that moment. If so, do it now.

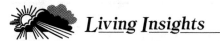 ## _Living Insights_

"You want me to do what, Lord?"

Ananias couldn't believe his ears. Sure, this was not your normal conversation in the first place, speaking with God, but go lay hands on Saul of Tarsus so he can regain his sight? Let that bully stay blind, Ananias may have thought. He deserves it.

But God said, "Go" a second time, and Ananias went. No more questions, arguments, or whining; he just departed. Was he scared? Probably. Wouldn't you have been? You don't forget the horror stories, the imprisonments, the threat of being dragged out of your home, or the beatings as a result of one conversation, even if it is with God. The terror of the persecution was still fresh on Ananias' mind. But he went anyway. Fears and all, he obeyed.

Has there ever been a time in your life when you didn't reach out to someone at a crossroads because of fear? For example, what if your best friend flirted with the idea of divorce? Would you have the courage to speak to him, encouraging him to stay committed? Or would you keep silent for fear of losing his friendship?

Maybe you know someone who's in the midst of a difficult turning point right now. And though God hasn't spoken to you in a vision, you still know there's something you should do. It's risky, you think. It probably won't be pleasant. Like Ananias, you can think of several reasons not to go. But the Spirit of God keeps prodding.

Are you running from something? Perhaps not, but for those of you who know exactly how Ananias must have felt because you're experiencing something similar right now, take a moment to reflect on what you think God is prompting you to do. Under the first heading, identify the other person(s) involved and the situation. Then, in the following section, write exactly what it is you feel God would have you do.

Situation

_____

_____

_____

_____

You Want Me to Do What, Lord?

_____

_____

_____

_____

_____

_____

As you struggle with whether or not to follow the Lord's leading in this, let me leave you with this helpful insight.

> [Courage] does not mean not being afraid. If we are not afraid it is the easiest thing in the world to do a thing. Real courage means being perfectly aware of the worst that can happen, being sickeningly afraid of it, and yet doing the *right* thing. . . . No man need ever be ashamed of being afraid; but he may well be ashamed of allowing his fear to stop him doing what in his heart of hearts he knows he ought to do.[4]

---

4. William Barclay, *The Gospel of John*, vol. 2, rev. ed., The Daily Study Bible Series (Philadelphia, Pa.: Westminster Press, 1975), p. 88.

Chapter 10

THE TURNING POINT OF GOD'S SOVEREIGNTY

Daniel 4; Romans 11:33–36

As then world heavyweight champion Muhammad Ali was just about to take off on an airplane flight, the stewardess came by and reminded him to fasten his seat belt. "Superman don't need no seat belt," Ali asserted. To which the quick-thinking stewardess replied, "Superman don't need no airplane, either." Ali fastened his belt.[1]

Sometimes it takes only a well-timed nudge to break through our fantasies of being omnipotent. Other times, however, it takes a powerhouse shove to dethrone the sovereign self, as it did with King Nebuchadnezzar.

Ruler of Babylon, the most powerful empire on earth at that time, Nebuchadnezzar was arrogant, self-confident, brutal, and definitely in charge. He was fast approaching a turning point, though, where he would learn that even his authority came from the hand of Another.

In Daniel 4, we find the king disturbed by a dream that baffled even his wisest advisors and mystics. After all the "magicians, the conjurers, the Chaldeans, and the diviners" came and went (v. 7), Daniel was finally consulted; and he not only interpreted the dream but also talked straight to the prideful heart of the dreamer.

> "'This is the interpretation, O king, and this is the decree of the Most High, which has come upon my lord the king: that you be driven away from mankind, and your dwelling place be with the beasts of the field, and you be given grass to eat like cattle and be drenched with the dew of heaven; and seven periods of time will pass over you, until you recognize

Parts of this lesson have been adapted from "God's Sovereignty," from the study guide *Stones of Remembrance*, coauthored by Ken Gire, from the Bible-teaching ministry of Charles R. Swindoll (Fullerton, Calif.: Insight for Living, 1988).

1. As told by Clifton Fadiman, ed., in *The Little, Brown Book of Anecdotes* (Boston, Mass.: Little, Brown and Co., 1985), p. 14.

that the Most High is ruler over the realm of mankind, and bestows it on whomever He wishes. And in that it was commanded to leave the stump with the roots of the tree, your kingdom will be assured to you after you recognize that it is Heaven that rules.'" (vv. 24–26)

Notice two key phrases in verses 25 and 26: "until you recognize" and "after you recognize." The word *acknowledge*, as the New International Version translates *recognize*, is a more precise rendering of the idea. Daniel is urging the king to accept and embrace, not just observe, the truth that "the Most High is ruler over the realm of mankind . . . that it is Heaven that rules."

Twelve months later, a gracious amount of time for God to give the unrepentant king, the prophecy was fulfilled.

"The king reflected and said, 'Is this not Babylon the great, which I myself have built as a royal residence by the might of my power and for the glory of my majesty?' While the word was in the king's mouth, a voice came from heaven, saying, 'King Nebuchadnezzar, to you it is declared: sovereignty has been removed from you, and you will be driven away from mankind, and your dwelling place will be with the beasts of the field. You will be given grass to eat like cattle, and seven periods of time will pass over you, until you recognize that the Most High is ruler over the realm of mankind, and bestows it on whomever He wishes.' Immediately the word concerning Nebuchadnezzar was fulfilled; and he was driven away from mankind and began eating grass like cattle, and his body was drenched with the dew of heaven, until his hair had grown like eagles' feathers and his nails like birds' claws." (vv. 30–33)

A long midnight of insanity descended on Nebuchadnezzar, until he acknowledged at last the sovereignty of God.

"But at the end of that period I, Nebuchadnezzar, raised my eyes toward heaven, and my reason returned to me, and I blessed the Most High and praised and honored Him who lives forever;
For His dominion is an everlasting dominion,

And His kingdom endures from generation to
    generation.
And all the inhabitants of the earth are
    accounted as nothing,
But He does according to His will in the host of
    heaven
And among the inhabitants of earth;
And no one can ward off His hand
Or say to Him, 'What hast Thou done?' . . .
Now I Nebuchadnezzar praise, exalt, and honor the
King of heaven, for all His works are true and His
ways just, and He is able to humble those who walk
in pride." (vv. 34–35, 37)

Like Nebuchadnezzar, whose reason returned only after he recognized the Lord's sovereignty, it is not until we embrace God's right to control that we will begin to think sanely and reason theologically.

Who Is in Charge?

God, who "does according to His will in the host of heaven And among the inhabitants of earth," is clearly in charge. Even when our world is a confusing mess? Yes, even then He is in control. For only He can fulfill the qualifications of sovereignty, which, if we listed them as in a résumé, would run something like this:

To be sovereign, one must . . .

- be absolutely powerful, infinitely wise, and completely objective

- see the end as clearly as the beginning

- have a clear and unbiased perspective at all times, never operating from prejudice

- entertain no fear; possess no ignorance; experience no frustration; have no needs, limitations, or restrictions

- have no match or rival on earth or in heaven

- always know what is best and pursue that goal consistently, never making a mistake

- be invincible, immutable, omnipotent, and self-sufficient

- have unsearchable judgments, unfathomable ways, and an unchangeable will

- be able to create rather than invent, direct rather than wish, control rather than suggest, guide rather than guess, fulfill rather than dream, and bring to a perfect conclusion rather than blindly hope for the best

Know anyone except God who comes near to qualifying for the job? Me neither.

What Does Sovereignty Mean . . . and Not Mean?

The apostle Paul's words at the end of Romans 11 are a fitting complement to our passage from Daniel.

> Oh, the depth of the riches both of the wisdom and knowledge of God! How unsearchable are His judgments and unfathomable His ways! (v. 33)

In other words, *our all-wise, all-knowing God reigns in realms beyond our comprehension to bring about a plan that is beyond our ability to hinder, alter, or stop.* In personalizing this definition, we would find that God's sovereignty encompasses all promotions as well as demotions, prosperity as well as adversity, tragedy as well as ecstasy, calamity as well as joy. It would envelop both illness and health, danger and safety, heartache and hope. When we cannot fathom why, He knows. When we cannot give reasons, He understands. When we cannot see the end, He is there.

Paul's doxology of praise crescendos in verses 34–36:

> For who has known the mind of the Lord, or who became His counselor? Or who has first given to Him that it might be paid back to him again? For from Him and through Him and to Him are all things. To Him be the glory forever. Amen.

Our sovereign Lord is Master and Mover, Giver and Receiver. He is the originator—"from Him"; the enforcer—"through Him"; the provider—"to Him."

This doctrine can bring much comfort to our anxious, worried hearts, but it can also be taken to unbiblical extremes. Some people allow themselves to become passive, lacking in evangelistic zeal and personal excellence. Yet notice the commands Paul issues on the heels of his doxology:

- Be transformed! (12:1–2)

- Exercise your spiritual gifts! (vv. 6–8)

- Develop loving relationships! (vv. 9–21)

- Be responsible! (13:1–7)

God's sovereignty does not release us from personal responsibility—including the responsibility for choosing our eternal destiny. Within the scope of God's reign we have the freedom to say yes or no to Christ.

Where Will This Lead?

Look again at the final words of Romans 11:36: "To Him be the glory forever. Amen." Everything leads back to His glory; He is the ultimate end, as 1 Corinthians 15:28 indicates.

> And when all things are subjected to Him, then the Son Himself also will be subjected to the One who subjected all things to Him, that God may be all in all.

Linger on that last phrase—"that God may be all in all." Not man. *God.* God will have His way; His will shall be accomplished. What seems frustrating and wrong and unfair now is not the end. It's just the turn of a chapter, not the close of God's book.

Why Do We Care?

Why is our recognition of God's sovereignty such a turning point? Why should we care about it so much? Three thoughts stand out.

First, *it relieves us of much of our anxiety.* We aren't consumed with trying to control the uncontrollable; rather, we learn to let God be God and trust Him in circumstances beyond our control.

Second, *it keeps us from being prideful.* When things are humming along nicely, it's easy to take credit for it. That's when we need to remember Nebuchadnezzar's lesson and humbly thank God for His grace.

And third, *it frees us from explaining.* We don't have to be the "Christian answer man" in the face of life's perplexities. Only God has all the answers, and we can rest in that. John Oxenham's poem "God's Handwriting" puts it like this:

> He writes in characters too grand
> For our short sight to understand;
> We catch but broken strokes, and try

To fathom all the mystery
Of withered hopes, of death, of life,
The endless war, the useless strife—
But there, with larger, clearer sight,
We shall see this—His way was right.[2]

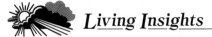 ## Living Insights
STUDY ONE

"God's in his heaven— / All's right with the world!" exulted the poet Robert Browning over a beautiful spring morning.[3] Unfortunately, many have taken these lines out of context to affirm God's sovereignty. But is that a true picture?

We read daily of violence, corruption, cruelty, betrayal, greed, and harm. God is indeed in heaven, but all is certainly not right with this world.

Is this a sign of some flaw in God's sovereignty? If you view His omnipotence as armor that should keep you from being pricked by the realities of life, then, yes, it would appear to be a chink. However, God's sovereignty is not meant to be armor; nor is it meant to be a panacea that sends you skipping along believing that, whatever happens, everything's going to turn out all right.

The sovereignty of the Lord is not easily understood or grasped. His judgments, as Paul said, are unsearchable and His ways, unfathomable (Rom. 11:33). But we can find peace amidst the mystery in knowing that at the heart of Him, He is good and He is love (1 John 4:8). And in searching for understanding, we need to recognize not only His sovereignty, but also the reality of personal responsibility. God's Word rings out with command after command, principle after principle for the way we should conduct ourselves and construct our lives. We are not passive marionettes in a divine puppet show; we are active participants in the building of God's kingdom. And we are that by God's grace and design.

Where are you concerning God's sovereignty? Have you struggled with reconciling it with the reality of evil?

---

2. John Oxenham, "God's Handwriting," as quoted by V. Raymond Edman in *The Disciplines of Life* (Minneapolis, Minn.: World Wide Publications, 1948), p. 166.

3. Robert Browning, "Song," from "Pippa Passes," in *Masterpieces of Religious Verse*, ed. James Dalton Morrison (New York, N.Y.: Harper and Brothers Publishers, 1948), no. 302.

What conclusions have you come to?

_____

_____

_____

_____

How do the truths of free will, choice, and personal responsibility impact your thinking?

_____

_____

_____

_____

For a better understanding of the relationship between God's sovereignty and personal responsibility, read chapter 13, "God's Sovereign Will and Decision Making," of Garry Friesen's *Decision Making and the Will of God* (Portland, Oreg.: Multnomah Press, 1980); Norman L. Geisler's *The Roots of Evil* (Grand Rapids, Mich.: Zondervan Publishing House; Richardson, Tex.: Probe Ministries International, 1978); and J. I. Packer's *Evangelism and the Sovereignty of God* (Downers Grove, Ill.: InterVarsity Press, 1977).

 Living Insights STUDY TWO

Knowing the character of our sovereign King makes it so much easier to let go of those things that really are beyond our power and to trust in God's help and plan. Take some time now to let your soul drink in the truths about God that flowed like a gentle spring rain from David's pen.

> I will extol Thee, my God, O King;
> And I will bless Thy name forever and ever. . . .
> The Lord is gracious and merciful;
> Slow to anger and great in lovingkindness.
> The Lord is good to all,
> And His mercies are over all His works. . . .

The Lord sustains all who fall,
And raises up all who are bowed down.
The eyes of all look to Thee,
And Thou dost give them their food in due time.
Thou dost open Thy hand,
And dost satisfy the desire of every living thing.
The Lord is righteous in all His ways,
And kind in all His deeds.
The Lord is near to all who call upon Him,
To all who call upon Him in truth.
He will fulfill the desire of those who fear Him;
He will also hear their cry and will save them.
The Lord keeps all who love Him;
But all the wicked, He will destroy.
My mouth will speak the praise of the Lord;
And all flesh will bless His holy name forever
    and ever.
(Ps. 145:1, 8–9, 14–21)

Chapter 11

DELIVERANCE
FROM DESPAIR

Selected Scriptures

The morning of August 24th was like any other in the ancient Roman city. Men and women, mothers and fathers went about business as usual, working hard in the bright sunlight while children romped beneath the cool shade of the mountain. Downtown, the temples of Venus, Apollo, Zeus, and Isis thrummed with the business of idol worship. The gods had been kind, the people believed, and the city prospered; so sacrifices for an even more prosperous future were being made. Yet, in a few fleeting hours, every man and woman, son and daughter would be dead—Mount Vesuvius would erupt and, in its fury, encase Pompeii in a tomb of lava for centuries to come.

About forty years before Pompeii was destroyed, another eruption took place in Jerusalem, the power of which caused all of heaven and earth to quake. It occurred on a Sunday during the predawn hours. The first to be shaken by it was a woman, Mary Magdalene. She came to the tomb of her beloved Master and was shocked to find the grave open and His body missing. Trembling with fear that someone had stolen Him, she panicked and took off running to find help (John 20:1–2). What she didn't know then was that the tomb had erupted with the power of God. The crucified Son of God had risen, triumphantly conquering death and bringing new life to a human race encased in sin.

Evidence for Jesus' Resurrection

Paul reasons in 1 Corinthians 15 that "if Christ has not been raised, your faith is worthless" (v. 17), and "if the dead are not raised, let us eat and drink, for tomorrow we die" (v. 32b). If Jesus did not rise from the dead, Christianity is no better than the pagan religions of Pompeii. But His triumph over the grave gives Christianity a unique distinctive: its founder *lives!*

Portions of this lesson have been adapted from the study guides *Jesus, Our Lord* (Fullerton, Calif.: Insight for Living, 1987) and *Beholding Christ . . . The Lamb of God: A Study of John 15–21* (Fullerton, Calif.: Insight for Living, 1987), both coauthored by Ken Gire, from the Bible-teaching ministry of Charles R. Swindoll.

Never once has objective evidence contradicted this proclamation. Never once have Paul or the early apostles been proven wrong—even by their critics. As Patrick Fairbairn rightly said, "The silence of the [critics] is as significant as the speech of the Christians."[1]

Why were the critics so silent? Because, frankly, they were stunned by the facts. Let's examine three key proofs that eloquently substantiate Christ's resurrection.

The Material Evidence

Exhibit A in this category is the *displaced stone* (see John 20:1). The door of Christ's tomb was a large, circular stone set on its edge and fitted into an inclined groove. It was not uncommon for such a stone to weigh a ton. Yet this in itself was not enough of a guarantee for the Pharisees that Jesus would never leave His grave. So they set an official seal on the stone and stationed a guard of Roman soldiers to discourage anyone from tampering with the tomb (see Matt. 27:62–66).

Who, then, could have moved the stone? The guards assigned to keep it secure? Of course not—to fail at their duty meant strict military discipline, possibly death. And certainly not the frightened and confused disciples either. Even if they had banded together, could a few fishermen and a tax accountant overpower ten to thirty trained Roman soldiers?

Exhibit B is the *empty tomb* (see John 20:2–4). Only three possible conclusions can account for this. First, some have suggested that Jesus didn't die on the cross; He only swooned. He was then put in the cool tomb where he later revived and then left. This theory sounds reasonable at first, until one looks at the facts. How could someone who was beaten, flogged, crucified, speared in the side, and even pronounced dead by His executioners suddenly revive, push a one-ton stone aside, overcome an entire Roman guard, and leave?

A second possible explanation is that the body was removed by either His friends or His enemies. If by enemies, what could their motive have been? And why would they remain silent when the preaching of Christ's resurrection hit the streets? To nip that rumor in the bud, all they had to do was parade Jesus' dead body down

---

1. As quoted by Josh McDowell in *Evidence That Demands a Verdict*, rev. ed. (San Bernardino, Calif.: Here's Life Publishers, 1979), p. 225.

the middle of Jerusalem. But they never did, because they didn't have it. If the body was taken by friends, how could they have slipped past the guards? Furthermore, it's incomprehensible that the disciples would have later died for Christ's cause—as all of them except perhaps John did—if the Resurrection were just a hoax and they knew it.

The third conclusion seems to be the only intelligent option: Christ's body left the tomb by supernatural means.

Upon coming to Jesus' tomb, Peter and John stumbled across another clue pointing to the Resurrection—Jesus' *grave clothes*, Exhibit C (see vv. 5–7). Along with this clue are several important references to the way John and Peter looked at the wrappings. The first is in verse 5— John *saw*. The Greek term used is *blepō*, meaning "to glance at something." John only glanced at the linen wrappings Jesus had been buried in. The second is in verse 6—Peter *beheld*. This comes from a different Greek term, *theōreō*, meaning "to take careful notice." Peter actually entered Jesus' tomb and stared wonderingly at the empty grave clothes. Why? J. N. D. Anderson explains.

> The Greek . . . seems to suggest that the linen clothes were lying, not strewn about the tomb, but where the body had been, and that there was a gap where the neck of Christ had lain—and that the napkin which had been about His head was not with the linen clothes but apart and wrapped in its own place, which I suppose means still done up, as though the body had simply withdrawn itself.[2]

The final reference to seeing occurs in verse 8. John followed Peter into the tomb and *saw* the grave clothes again. Only this time the word used is *horaō*, which means "to get a mental picture, to realize what has taken place." According to John Stott, when John saw that the grave clothes "had been neither touched nor folded nor manipulated by any human being," and that "they were like a discarded chrysalis from which the butterfly has emerged,"[3] he suddenly realized what had occurred—Jesus was resurrected!

---

2. As quoted by McDowell in *Evidence That Demands a Verdict*, p. 220.

3. As quoted by McDowell in *Evidence That Demands a Verdict*, p. 220.

Physical Appearances of Jesus

Providing further proof are Christ's post-resurrection appearances. The New Testament records no less than eleven physical encounters with the risen Christ. It has been theorized that these were merely grief-induced hallucinations. But the fact that these encounters occurred at different times, in different places, with a variety of individuals makes the theory itself seem to be the hallucination. In fact, on one occasion, Jesus appeared to more than five hundred people (see 1 Cor. 15:6). For so many people to have shared the same hallucination at the same time strains the imagination far more than the probability of Christ's bodily resurrection.

Incredible Transformation of the Disciples

The third key piece of evidence that stunned the critics into silence was the amazing transformation that took place in the disciples. At the time of Christ's arrest and crucifixion, they had scattered like scared sheep (see Matt. 26:56). However, after they had seen the risen Christ and been filled by the Holy Spirit, this weak-kneed band of deserters became bold witnesses who turned the world upside down (see Acts 17:6). Even Peter, who denied Christ so emphatically, preached unashamedly about Him in the very city where He was only recently executed (2:14–36).

Verdict That Frees Us from Despair

To live without faith in the Resurrection is to deny overwhelming evidence. To die without hope in the Resurrection is to face a barren eternity. What could be more bleak? But Jesus can deliver us from that despair. His resurrection was the premier showing of God's power over sin and death, a preview of the coming attractions Jesus promised to those who believe in Him: "Because I live, you shall live also" (John 14:19b).

Frank Morison didn't believe that. He was, in fact, so confident in his unbelief that this well-educated British lawyer set out to write a book disproving Christ's resurrection. When he sat down to sift through the historical data, he came with his magnifying glass and his twenty questions—a skeptical Sherlock Holmes. He also came facing a barren eternity without hope. However, when he finished cross-examining the biblical evidence, he left the courtroom a convinced man. He concludes his book by stating:

There may be, and, as the writer thinks, there certainly is, a deep and profoundly historical basis for that much disputed sentence in the Apostles' Creed— "The *third day* he rose again from the dead."[4]

If your jury is still deliberating on whether Jesus rose from the dead, carefully sift through the evidence yourself. After all, if there is anything to be certain about, it should be the resurrection of Christ, our only deliverance from despair.[5]

Living Insights

Substantiating the Resurrection with the clues left behind is a fascinating study. But now let's move beyond just the facts and personalize the impact Christ's empty tomb has on our lives. In this Living Insight and the next, let Eugene Peterson lead you in this effort with two of his devotions from his book *Praying with Jesus*.

Read through John 20:1–18 to begin.

"I Have Seen the Lord"

> Jesus said to her, "Woman, why are you weeping? Whom are you looking for?" Supposing him to be the gardener, she said to him, "Sir, if you have carried him away, tell me where you have laid him, and I will take him away." Jesus said to her, "Mary!" She turned and said to him in Hebrew, "Rabbouni!" (which means Teacher).
>
> *John 20:15–16*

Mary is emptied of expectation and devoid of hope. Every tie to Jesus is broken and every link to Jesus severed. Out of such emptiness and loss comes the fulfillment of God's promises. "Only where graves are is resurrection" (Nietzsche).

---

4. Frank Morison, *Who Moved the Stone?* (1930; reprint, Grand Rapids, Mich.: Zondervan Publishing House, Lamplighter Books, 1958), p. 193.

5. For further study, see *Who Moved the Stone?* by Frank Morison and *Evidence That Demands a Verdict* by Josh McDowell.

What sorrow separates you from God?[6]

_____

_____

_____

PRAYER: Lord Jesus Christ, I think because you are
not where I expect you that you are not anywhere;
I think that because you do not appear in the way
I last saw you that you are not to be seen. And you,
praise God, are always surprising me with a resurrection appearance. _Amen._[7]

_____

_____

_____

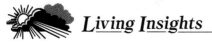 ## _Living Insights_   STUDY TWO

Begin this devotion by prayerfully reading John 21:1–8.

"It Is the Lord!"

> Just after daybreak, Jesus stood on the beach;
> but the disciples did not know that it was
> Jesus. Jesus said to them, "Children, you have
> no fish, have you?" They answered him,
> "No." He said to them, "Cast the net to the
> right side of the boat, and you will find
> some."
>
> _John 21:4–6_

The sunrise appearance of Jesus breaks in upon our
lives with explosive force. Work that was futile apart
from Christ becomes successful in his presence.

_____

6. Eugene H. Peterson, _Praying with Jesus: A Year of Daily Prayers and Reflections on the Words and
Actions of Jesus_ (San Francisco, Calif.: HarperSanFrancisco, 1993), reading for December 23.

7. Peterson, _Praying with Jesus_, reading for December 23.

How did Peter know it was Jesus?[8]

_____

_____

_____

PRAYER: Your resurrection life, Lord Jesus, is like a sunrise in work that has lost meaning and in routines that have become pointless. Whatever my work today, I will do it in the recognition of your presence, and under your command. _Amen._[9]

_____

_____

_____

8. Peterson, _Praying with Jesus_, reading for December 27.
9. Peterson, _Praying with Jesus_, reading for December 27.

Chapter 12

GOD'S AMAZING GRACE

Selected Scriptures

Who am I?

My godly mother died when I was a young child. Reared by a sea-captain father, taken to sea at age eleven, I soon forgot the Scriptures she had taught me.

Several years later, I was pressed into the British navy and became a midshipman. By then I had earned the reputation of being able to curse for two hours straight without repeating a word. Restless and wild, I tried to desert, was caught, stripped, whipped severely, and degraded to the ranks. I eventually ran away to Africa, but only so "I might sin my fill."

And I did.

Debauched and distant from God, I fell into the hands of a Portuguese slave trader. For months the chief woman of the trader's harem treated me like an animal, beating me and forcing me to grovel in the dirt for my food.

Reduced to a mangy cur of a man, I finally escaped and made my way to the shores of Africa. Picked up by a passing ship, I earned the position of first mate because I was a skilled navigator. But while the captain was ashore one day, I broke out the ship's rum and got the entire crew drunk. When the captain came back, he was so furious he hit me, knocking me overboard.

I would have drowned were it not for a sailor who pulled me back on board by spearing my thigh with a boat hook. The wound was so large that it left a scar big enough to put my fist in. Some weeks later, when the ship neared the coast of Scotland, it sailed into a storm and almost sank. For days I manned the pumps below deck in what seemed a hopeless nightmare.

It was then that I desperately called out to God. He answered my helpless cry, and I emerged from the hold of that ship to later become the chaplain of England's Parliament and even to preach before the king. I am the vile blasphemer whom many would subsequently refer to as the second founder of the Church of England. And it was I who wrote:

Amazing grace! how sweet the sound,

That saved a wretch like me!
I once was lost, but now am found,
    Was blind, but now I see.

These were the lyrics born out of my wayward, free-versed life. And to my ears, there is no sweeter sound than grace in all the world.

Who am I? John Newton.[1]

Newton's pilgrimage to Christ was indeed extreme and unique. But the basis of his salvation was no different from any other Christian's—the grace of God. What is grace? God's undeserved, unlimited favor poured out on sinners, which we could never earn, will never deserve, and can never repay. No wonder Newton called it "amazing."

The apostle Paul's journey to finding Christ, like Newton's, was also extreme and unique. And he, too, wrote of God's amazing grace in what is known as the Magna Charta of Christian doctrine: the book of Romans. In chapter 3, for example, we're told that "all have sinned and fall short of the glory of God" (v. 23). Against such a black backdrop, he then sets forth the wonderful news that we are

> justified as a gift by His grace through the redemp-
> tion which is in Christ Jesus. (v. 24)

A little later in chapter 5, Paul again recounts our rescue from sin by God's grace.

> But God demonstrates His own love toward us, in that
> while we were yet sinners, Christ died for us. (v. 8)

Isn't God's unmerited favor incredible? Without it, we would all be "lost" and "blind," as Newton put it. By His grace, however, we are found, we see the light of Christ and believe (see also Eph. 2:4–9).

But that's not all! The amazing grace that saved us remains our constant companion, just as Jay Kesler discovered in his own walk with Christ.

> I'm more aware of my need of grace. I'm afraid that

---

1. Lyrics to "Amazing Grace" and story of John Newton are taken from Donald Grey Barnhouse's God's Grace: Romans 5:12-21, a 3 vols. in 1 edition (1959; reprint, Grand Rapids, Mich.: William B. Eerdmans Publishing Co., 1973), pp. 127–29; and Amos R. Wells' A Treasury of Hymn Stories (1945; reprint, Grand Rapids, Mich.: Baker Book House, 1992), p. 294.

I once wanted to arrive at the gate of heaven with no need of it because of my personal piety and perfection. I've given up on that. To be involved means failure, misunderstanding, and sin as well as victories and accomplishment. Grace is not the enemy, but a friend for which I am grateful.[2]

Grace is not simply a one-time acquaintance at salvation; it becomes our loyal friend for life. Passing patron or intimate ally—which perception best characterizes your view of grace? If you've always associated God's favor only with salvation, then come with us as we explore its ongoing presence in our lives.

A Friend at What Times in My Life?

The close-knit bond of grace is felt in at least three specific times in everyone's life.

First: When I Am Hurting

Because of the surpassing greatness of the revelations, for this reason, to keep me from exalting myself, there was given me a thorn in the flesh, a messenger of Satan to buffet me—to keep me from exalting myself! Concerning this I entreated the Lord three times that it might depart from me. And He has said to me, "My grace is sufficient for you, for power is perfected in weakness." Most gladly, therefore, I will rather boast about my weaknesses, that the power of Christ may dwell in me. Therefore I am well content with weaknesses, with insults, with distresses, with persecutions, with difficulties, for Christ's sake; for when I am weak, then I am strong. (2 Cor. 12:7–10)

We don't know what Paul's "thorn in the flesh" actually was, nor do we need to. What's important is that he suffered just like we do. The thorn pierced him deeply, constantly reminding him of his inadequacy. It spawned fears, raised doubts, perhaps even caused physical pain. And at those moments when Paul felt the most

2. Jay Kesler, as quoted by Lloyd Cory, comp., in *Quotable Quotations* (Wheaton, Ill.: Scripture Press Publications, Victor Books, 1985), pp. 163–64.

worthless, did the Father condemn him because of his weakness? No! Grace accepts and understands. It provides comfort, not criticism. It reaches out to support, not to tear down. Grace is our enthusiastic ally, the one who makes us sufficient in the midst of our weakness and pain. Grace is our friend.

Second: When I Am Weak . . . Unable to Stand Firm

> For we do not have a high priest who cannot sympathize with our weaknesses, but one who has been tempted in all things as we are, yet without sin. Let us therefore draw near with confidence to the throne of grace, that we may receive mercy and may find grace to help in time of need. (Heb. 4:15–16)

Temptation stalks everyone. It never quits, never tires of assaulting its victims until it finds a weakness or wears us down, and then it comes in for the kill. Nothing leaves us feeling more helpless and ashamed than the repeated onslaughts of a powerful temptation. And we feel discouraged, like we're always giving ground in a losing battle. We're weak, tired, ready to quit. What are we supposed to do?

Come to the throne of grace, Christ beckons. Don't be afraid. He understands what you're going through, He remembers the struggle. Draw near and He will grant you the same strength that rescued Him in His time of need.

Third: Grace That Keeps Me from Succumbing to Unprincipled Men

> You therefore, beloved, knowing this beforehand, be on your guard lest, being carried away by the error of unprincipled men, you fall from your own steadfastness, but grow in the grace and knowledge of our Lord and Savior Jesus Christ. To Him be the glory, both now and to the day of eternity. Amen. (2 Pet. 3:17–18)

Steadfastness is that straight-and-narrow tightrope we must all walk "in the midst of a crooked and perverse generation" (see Phil. 2:15b). But how? To keep from falling, Peter says we must maintain a balanced growth in the grace and knowledge of our Lord. "How easy it is to grow in knowledge but not in grace!" Warren Wiersbe warns:

> All of us know far more of the Bible than we really live. Knowledge without grace is a terrible weapon,

and grace without knowledge can be very shallow. But when we combine grace and knowledge, we have a marvelous tool for building our lives and for building the church.[3]

Growing in grace means becoming more like Jesus. Take a look at the Christlike qualities Peter mentions in 2 Peter 1:5–7, and you'll see the different facets of His character that are produced in us by His unmerited, unstoppable, transforming grace. Seek to know and obey Him, and "the God of all grace, who called you to His eternal glory in Christ, will Himself perfect, confirm, strengthen and establish you" (1 Pet. 5:10b). Now that's amazing!

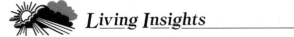 **Living Insights**   STUDY ONE

Have there been times when you sensed, more than others, the befriending presence of God's grace? If you need an encouraging reminder, use the three occasions noted in the lesson to write out the significant details of how His grace ministered to you.

When I Was Hurting . . .

_____

_____

_____

_____

When I Was Weak, Unable to Stand . . .

_____

_____

_____

_____

3. Warren W. Wiersbe, *Be Alert* (Wheaton, Ill.: Scripture Press Publications, Victor Books, 1984), p. 99.

When I Could Have Succumbed to Unprincipled People . . .

_____

_____

_____

_____

Living Insights STUDY TWO

As we bring our entire study to a close, take one last look at the topics covered in all twelve chapters and briefly summarize the key points you've learned from each.

Shedding Light on Our Dark Side

_____

_____

Pride: The Absence of Humility

_____

_____

Lust: Sex Out of Control

_____

_____

A Careful Analysis of the Unborn

_____

_____

In Defense of the Helpless

_____

_____

Celebrate the Feast!

Curing the Plague of Death

Claiming the Promise of Life

Life's Turning Points

The Turning Point of God's Sovereignty

Deliverance from Despair

God's Amazing Grace

BOOKS FOR
PROBING FURTHER

For further illumination on our dark side and God's healing light, here are some excellent resources.

Getting Sex under Control

Grant, George, and Mark A. Horne. *Legislating Immorality: The Homosexual Movement Comes Out of the Closet.* Chicago, Ill.: Moody Press; Franklin, Tenn.: Legacy Communications, 1993. This book bears the warning that some of the material presented may not be suitable for young or sensitive readers.

Perkins, Bill. *Fatal Attractions: Overcoming Our Secret Addictions.* Eugene, Oreg.: Harvest House Publishers, 1991.

Stafford, Tim. *Sexual Chaos.* Revised edition of *The Sexual Christian.* Downers Grove, Ill.: InterVarsity Press, 1993.

Protecting the Unborn

Campolo, Tony, and Gordon Aeschliman. *50 Ways You Can Be Pro-life.* Downers Grove, Ill.: InterVarsity Press, 1993.

Geisler, Norman L. "The Natural Right." In *In Search of a National Morality*, edited by William Bentley Ball. Grand Rapids, Mich.: Baker Book House; San Francisco, Calif.: Ignatius Press, 1992.

Koop, C. Everett. *The Right to Live: The Right to Die.* Wheaton, Ill.: Tyndale House Publishers, 1980.

Powell, John. *Abortion: The Silent Holocaust.* Allen, Tex.: Tabor Publishing, 1981.

Sproul, R. C. *Abortion: A Rational Look at an Emotional Issue.* Colorado Springs, Colo.: NavPress, 1990.

Swindoll, Charles R. *Sanctity of Life.* Dallas, Tex.: Word Publishing, 1990.

Defending the Helpless

Heitritter, Lynn, and Jeanette Vought. *Helping Victims of Sexual Abuse*. Minneapolis, Minn.: Bethany House Publishers, 1989.

Huskey, Alice. *Stolen Childhood: What You Need to Know about Sexual Abuse*. Downers Grove, Ill.: InterVarsity Press, 1990.

Johnson, Karen Cecilia. *Through the Tears: Caring for the Sexually Abused Child*. Nashville, Tenn.: Broadman Press, 1993.

Morrison, Jan. *A Safe Place: Beyond Sexual Abuse*. Wheaton, Ill.: Harold Shaw Publishers, 1990. This excellent resource is directed primarily to teens.

Finding Hope in the Resurrection

McDowell, Josh. *The Resurrection Factor*. San Bernardino, Calif.: Here's Life Publishers, 1981.

Marshall, Peter. *The First Easter*. 1959. Reprint. Old Tappan, N.J.: Fleming H. Revell Co., Chosen Books, 1987.

Morison, Frank. *Who Moved the Stone?* 1930. Reprint. Grand Rapids, Mich.: Zondervan Publishing House, Lamplighter Books, 1958.

All of the books listed above are recommended reading; however, some may be out of print and available only through a library. For books currently available, please contact your local Christian bookstore. Works by Charles R. Swindoll are available through Insight for Living. IFL also offers some books by other authors— please note the Ordering Information that follows and contact the office which serves you.

NOTES

NOTES

NOTES

NOTES